3000 Powerful Questions About Myself

3000 Powerful Questions About Myself

Insightful Questions for Personal Reflection and Self-Discovery

Be.Bull Publishing Group
Mauricio Vasquez

Toronto, Canada

Authors:

Be.Bull Publishing Group

Mauricio Vasquez

First Printing: May 2024

ISBN 978-1-998402-25-0 Hardcover book
ISBN 978-1-998402-26-7 Paperback
ISBN 978-1-998402-27-4 Ebook

Introduction

Questions are the keys that unlock new knowledge, insights, and understanding. They challenge us, inspire curiosity, and open the door to exploration. "3000 Powerful Questions About Myself" is a book designed not only to engage and entertain but to delve deep into the introspective journey of self-discovery.

Why is exploring personal questions important for your growth and self-awareness?

Foremost, engaging with introspective questions helps to clarify who you are, what you value, and where you want to go in life. This book provides a structured path for reflecting on various aspects of your life and identity—from your dreams and fears to your beliefs and relationships. Each question is a steppingstone towards deeper self-knowledge and personal clarity.

In today's fast-paced world, taking the time to pause and reflect is more valuable than ever. By exploring these questions, you invite introspection that fosters growth and self-understanding. Whether you use these questions as a daily journaling prompt, a tool for meditation, or as conversation starters with loved ones, they inspire thought and encourage a deeper connection with your inner self.

This book covers a wide array of themes, ensuring that every facet of life is addressed—from the mundane to the profound. It challenges you to confront your assumptions, examine your motives, and uncover your hidden desires. The questions not only encourage you to think, but also to feel, reflect, and react.

What if you discover new things about yourself? What if these questions reveal dreams you were too apprehensive to pursue or fears you've hidden deep inside? The potential for transformation and enlightenment is significant. But, more importantly, this journey of questions is about embracing the totality of who you are.

Here's a thought that resonates deeply with the purpose of this book:

"It is not the answers that enlighten, but the questions." – Decouvertes.

You need not worry about finding the time or the right way to explore these questions—I have curated this extensive list to facilitate a smooth and reflective journey through your inner landscape.

"3000 Powerful Questions About Myself" equips you to embark on a profound exploration of your life's narrative, enhancing not just your self-awareness but potentially transforming your outlook on life. Let's begin this journey together, one question at a time.

Table de Contents

Guidelines for Asking Powerful Questions 9

Tips for the Use of This Book...10

Topics 12

    PERSONAL IDENTITY QUESTIONS...12

    LIFE EXPERIENCES QUESTIONS..13

    VALUES AND BELIEFS QUESTIONS 15

    DREAMS AND ASPIRATIONS QUESTIONS 16

    RELATIONSHIPS AND SOCIAL LIFE QUESTIONS 18

    CAREER AND EDUCATION QUESTIONS 19

    HOBBIES AND INTERESTS QUESTIONS 21

    TRAVEL AND ADVENTURE QUESTIONS 22

    HEALTH AND WELLBEING QUESTIONS 24

    FAVORITES AND PREFERENCES QUESTIONS..................................25

    TECHNOLOGY AND MEDIA QUESTIONS..27

    SELF-HELP AND PERSONAL DEVELOPMENT QUESTIONS 28

    EDUCATION AND LEARNING QUESTIONS 30

    CREATIVITY AND INNOVATION QUESTIONS 32

    FINANCIAL ATTITUDES QUESTIONS...33

    CULTURAL HERITAGE QUESTIONS...35

    LIFE MILESTONES QUESTIONS...36

    DECISION MAKING QUESTIONS 39

    MINDFULNESS AND SPIRITUALITY QUESTIONS................................41

    ENVIRONMENTAL AWARENESS QUESTIONS 42

    ART AND CULTURE QUESTIONS...44

    COMMUNITY AND SOCIETY QUESTIONS 45

    LEADERSHIP AND MANAGEMENT QUESTIONS 47

    MUSIC AND ENTERTAINMENT QUESTIONS 48

    HISTORICAL INFLUENCES QUESTIONS 50

    COMEDY AND HUMOR QUESTIONS 51

    FOOD AND CUISINE QUESTIONS...53

FITNESS AND SPORTS QUESTIONS 54

PERSONAL CHALLENGES QUESTIONS 56

PETS AND ANIMALS QUESTIONS 57

SCIENCE AND INNOVATION QUESTIONS 59

FANTASY AND IMAGINATION QUESTIONS 61

FASHION AND STYLE QUESTIONS 62

GAMES AND RECREATION QUESTIONS 64

HEALTH AND SAFETY QUESTIONS 65

PARENTING AND FAMILY LIFE QUESTIONS 67

FUTURE AND TECHNOLOGY QUESTIONS 68

BOOKS AND LITERATURE QUESTIONS 70

LANGUAGE AND COMMUNICATION QUESTIONS 71

TRAVEL AND EXPLORATION QUESTIONS 73

VOLUNTEERING AND CHARITY QUESTIONS 74

LAW AND JUSTICE QUESTIONS 76

INTERNET AND SOCIAL MEDIA QUESTIONS 78

RETIREMENT AND AGING QUESTIONS 79

BUSINESS AND ENTREPRENEURSHIP QUESTIONS 81

HOLIDAYS AND FESTIVITIES QUESTIONS 82

MORAL AND ETHICAL DILEMMAS QUESTIONS 84

GLOBAL ISSUES AND AWARENESS QUESTIONS 85

INNOVATION AND FUTURE TRENDS QUESTIONS 87

DEATH AND AFTERLIFE QUESTIONS 88

Final Words 90

A Quick Favor to Ask 93

Guidelines for Asking Powerful Questions

This section provides you with guidelines for asking powerful questions that foster self-discovery and personal insight. Use these questions to help you explore the depths of your inner self and bring clarity to your thoughts and feelings. Understanding how to engage with these questions effectively will enhance your journey through "3000 Powerful Questions About Myself".

Crafting and Engaging with Powerful Questions:

1. Encourage Deep Reflection: Opt for open-ended questions that provoke deeper thinking. These questions should elicit comprehensive answers that go beyond simple 'yes' or 'no' responses. They should encourage you to ponder, evaluate, and analyze your beliefs, decisions, and feelings.

2. Facilitate Personal Insights: Powerful questions should help you uncover and address your own needs, fears, and desires. The goal is to enable a deeper understanding of your personal motivations and the factors shaping your life choices.

3. Prompt Authenticity: Ask questions in a way that encourages genuine and honest responses. Frame the questions in a way that makes you feel safe and open, allowing you to express your true feelings and thoughts without fear of judgment.

4. Focus on Self-Benefit: While in other contexts, questions might aim to benefit others, in this personal journaling scenario, the focus is on your growth and development. Each question should be a tool for your own self-improvement, helping you to better understand and articulate your personal journey.

5. Encourage Exploration of Emotions: Engage questions that prompt you to explore and articulate your emotions. Understanding how you feel about certain experiences or decisions is crucial for personal development.

6. Shift Perspectives from Problems to Solutions: When facing personal dilemmas or challenges, frame questions that help shift your focus from dwelling on problems to exploring potential solutions and positive outcomes.

7. Ensure Non-Judgmental Framing: Craft questions in a non-judgmental tone to prevent any self-defensive reactions. Avoid questions that start with "why" which can sometimes lead to justifications rather than introspection.

8. Avoid Leading Questions: Ensure that questions are open and unbiased, not leading you to any predetermined answer. This maintains the integrity of your self-discovery process, helping you to uncover your true thoughts and beliefs.

9. Keep Questions Simple and Clear: Clarity and simplicity in questioning can be more impactful. Complex or overly detailed questions can distract or overwhelm. Simple questions often lead straight to the core, promoting clearer and more focused introspection.

10. Use Questions as a Gateway for Further Reflection: Let each question be a starting point for deeper exploration. After answering a question, consider why you answered the way you did and what that reveals about your character, life situation, or experiences.

These guidelines make your interaction with "3000 Powerful Questions About Myself" as enriching and insightful as possible. As you progress through these questions, you will build a more detailed and profound understanding of who you are and what shapes your view of the world.

Tips for the Use of This Book

"3000 Powerful Questions About Myself" facilitates a profound journey into self-discovery and personal reflection. Consider the following tips on effectively using this book to maximize the benefits of this journey.

1. Diverse Categories for Flexible Exploration: Questions are organized into diverse categories to cover various aspects of life and self. While categories provide a structured approach, many questions universally apply. Feel free to jump between sections as inspired.

2. Emphasize Reflective Listening: When discussing these questions with others, focus on listening attentively. Pay attention not only to words but also to emotions and nonverbal cues. This enhances understanding and deepens the connection between conversational partners.

3. Personalize Your Approach: Tailor questions to your current life context or specific areas of introspection. Modify or adapt questions to suit your reflective needs or to spark further curiosity about yourself.

4. Engage Creatively: Questions are open-ended, providing a platform for creative engagement. Interpret these questions in ways that spark your imagination or fit your personal narrative.

5. Encourage Follow-up Questions: Use initial answers as springboards for deeper exploration. Asking follow-up questions based on your responses can uncover deeper insights and reflections.

6. Simplicity and Clarity: To avoid confusion and maintain focus, ask one question at a time. Keep your inquiries clear and to the point, ensuring that they are easy to understand and reflect upon.

7. Adapt Questions to Your Voice: While the questions provided serve as a guide, adapting them to your own style and vocabulary can make the process more natural and engaging.

8. Document Your Answers: Consider writing down your answers or keeping a journal. This not only tracks your progress, but also helps in revisiting thoughts and observing how your perspectives develop over time.

9. Use Questions as Daily Prompts: Integrate questions into your daily routine. Starting or ending your day with a reflective question can provide meaningful bookends to your daily experiences.

10. Share and Discuss: Share your insights with friends or family where comfortable. Discussing your answers can provide new perspectives and deepen relationships through shared understanding and vulnerability.

By incorporating these tips, "3000 Powerful Questions About Myself" becomes more than just a book; it transforms into a tool for meaningful self-exploration and personal growth. Each question is an opportunity to learn more about yourself and to articulate the narrative of your life with greater clarity and depth.

Topics

PERSONAL IDENTITY QUESTIONS

1. What three words would you use to describe yourself to a stranger?
2. If you could change one decision in your past, what would it be and why?
3. What are you most proud of achieving in your life so far?
4. What fear have you overcome, and how did you do it?
5. What is a belief you held strongly as a child that you still uphold today?
6. Which of your personality traits has been the most beneficial in your life?
7. If you could solve one personal problem, what would it be?
8. What song best represents your life journey up to this point?
9. What is the most valuable lesson you've learned from a family member?
10. If you could write a letter to your future self, what would you say?
11. What part of your daily routine do you look forward to most?
12. Which book has had the most significant impact on your views or personality?
13. What is one thing you've always wanted to learn but haven't yet?
14. What does the concept of "home" mean to you?
15. How do you handle situations that take you out of your comfort zone?
16. What is one personal trait you would like to improve, and what steps could you take to get there?
17. In what ways do you think others misunderstand you?
18. What moment in your life would make the perfect movie scene?
19. What quote or saying do people associate with you?
20. What are you most grateful for at this stage of your life?
21. What do you want people to remember about you?
22. How do you define success, and do you feel you've achieved it?
23. What part of your life do you feel most in control of?
24. What is your earliest memory of feeling wonder?
25. Who has been your biggest influence in shaping your values?
26. What kind of situations make you feel most alive?
27. What is one unpopular opinion you hold, and why do you think you feel this way?
28. What accomplishment are you secretly proud of?
29. What aspect of your life do you think you lead by example?
30. How have your dreams and goals changed over the past ten years?
31. What is the most important piece of advice you would give your younger self?
32. What do you do to improve your mood when you feel down?
33. When was the last time you pushed beyond your comfort zone, and what was the result?
34. How do you deal with someone who views the world differently than you?
35. What are the top three qualities you admire in others?
36. What does your ideal day look like from morning to night?

37. What are the most significant changes you've seen in yourself over the last five years?

38. What motivates you to get up in the morning?

39. What fictional character do you most relate to, and why?

40. How do you think your friends would describe you in three words?

41. What do you think is your most misunderstood emotion?

42. What challenge are you currently facing, and how are you dealing with it?

43. What is one life lesson you have learned from a mistake?

44. What do you consider your greatest strength, and how has it helped you?

45. When do you feel you're most vulnerable, and what does that tell you about yourself?

46. How do you prioritize your mental and physical health?

47. What aspect of your life would you like to simplify?

48. What was the last new thing you tried, and what did it teach you?

49. What is the biggest risk you've ever taken, and what was the outcome?

50. How do you express love, and how do you prefer to receive it?

51. What is something you've done that has made a significant impact on someone else's life?

52. What is one thing that you think makes you unique to everyone else?

53. How has your perspective on the world changed in the last year?

54. What is a habit you have now that you wish you had started much earlier?

55. What do you wish people knew about you without you having to tell them?

56. What is the hardest truth you've had to accept?

57. What do you most often look forward to when you have time alone?

58. How has your upbringing influenced your outlook on life?

59. What is one change you could make to your lifestyle that you believe would give you more peace?

60. When looking at your life right now, what feels like it's missing, and why do you think that is?

LIFE EXPERIENCES QUESTIONS

1. What is the most significant challenge you've overcome in your life?

2. Describe when you felt completely at peace. What was happening?

3. Can you recall a time when you laughed so hard you cried? What was so funny?

4. What is the best advice you've ever received and who gave it to you?

5. What experience changed your outlook on life?

6. Describe the most adventurous thing you've ever done.

7. When have you felt the most scared?

8. What is your happiest childhood memory?

9. What has been your biggest disappointment, and how did you handle it?

10. What life event are you most proud of experiencing?

11. Have you ever experienced a "miracle"? What happened?

12. What was the most stressful situation you've been in? How did you manage it?

13. What is one life lesson you learned the hard way?

14. Describe a time when you met someone who changed your life.

15. What is the most unusual place you have visited?

16. What personal habits are you most proud of developing?

17. Who has been the kindest to you in your life?

18. What was your first job, and what did you learn from it?

19. Recall a time you made a tough decision that turned out to be correct.

20. What was your first major purchase, and why did you choose it?

21. What is the best vacation you've ever taken?

22. Describe a moment when you stood up for something you believed in.

23. What is the most important tradition you want to pass on?

24. Recall when something seemingly insignificant affected your life.

25. What was your favorite age growing up, and why?

26. What is a skill you learned as a child that you still use today?

27. When did you feel that you truly became an adult?

28. What is the most meaningful gift you've ever received?

29. Describe a time you failed at something important to you. What did you learn?

30. What was the most peaceful day you ever had?

31. What's a question you wish people would ask about your life?

32. Who or what has been your biggest teacher in life?

33. Describe a small, everyday moment that holds enormous significance to you.

34. What is a tradition from your childhood that you continue today?

35. What was the first concert you attended? Describe the experience.

36. Which historical event had the biggest impact on your family?

37. Describe a time you felt most connected to your family.

38. What's the bravest thing you've ever done?

39. What's the longest road trip you've ever taken, and what did you learn from it?

40. Which book have you read that made you feel like it was written just for you?

41. What is one thing you did to step out of your comfort zone?

42. How have your priorities changed over the years?

43. What's the most important lesson you've learned from a foreign culture?

44. What is the most humbling experience you've ever had?

45. Describe the moment you realized what you wanted to do with your life.

46. What unexpected turn did your life take, and where did it lead you?

47. What was your most memorable birthday and why?

48. Have you ever lost something important to you and found it later? What was it?

49. Describe your most cherished family heirloom and its story.

50. What was a typical day like for you ten years ago?

51. What is the hardest work you've ever done, physically or emotionally?

52. What personal change have you made that you are most proud of?

53. What is the kindest thing a stranger has ever done for you?

54. Describe a time when you felt most misunderstood.

55. What is the best part about your life right now?

56. What historical period do you wish you could have experienced?

57. What personal crisis turned out to be a blessing in disguise?

58. What is the greatest piece of wisdom you've learned from your parents?

59. What is one thing you still want to check off your bucket list?

60. Share a time when someone or something completely took you out of your comfort zone.

VALUES AND BELIEFS QUESTIONS

1. What core value do you believe every person should possess?

2. How have your beliefs changed as you have aged?

3. What ethical dilemma has challenged you the most?

4. When faced with uncertainty, what moral compass guides you?

5. What belief have you defended most vigorously?

6. What does honesty mean to you in daily life?

7. How do you determine if someone is trustworthy?

8. What cultural value from your heritage influences you the most?

9. What is the biggest sacrifice you've made for someone else?

10. How do you reconcile differences between your beliefs and those of your family?

11. What value do you most appreciate in your friendships?

12. Which historical figure embodies values you admire?

13. How do you practice forgiveness in your life?

14. What belief about life do you think everyone should have?

15. How do your values influence your career choices?

16. What do you believe is the purpose of your life?

17. How do you balance personal happiness and societal expectations?

18. What does the concept of duty mean to you?

19. How has your upbringing shaped your values today?

20. What role does faith play in your life?

21. What act of kindness has had the longest-lasting impact on you?

22. What do you value most in a leader?

23. How do you apply your beliefs in your daily interactions?

24. What lesson about life have you learned the hard way?

25. How do you handle situations that test your values?

26. What does it mean for you to live a good life?

27. What belief or habit has improved your life the most?

28. What tradition do you hold on to that reflects your beliefs?

29. How do you respond to people who question your beliefs?

30. What is one belief that you think would improve society if everyone adopted it?

31. How do you practice self-discipline, and why do you think it's important?

32. What values do you want to pass on to your children or future generations?

33. How do you define justice, and have you ever fought for it?

34. What does freedom mean to you, personally and socially?

35. How do you decide what is right and wrong?

36. What does it mean for you to be a good friend?

37. How do you approach conflicts between your personal interests and ethical obligations?

38. What is the most important lesson you've taught someone else?

39. How do you deal with betrayal, and what belief helps you move forward?

40. How do you prioritize your responsibilities to yourself, your family, and your community?

41. In what ways do you challenge your own beliefs?

42. How has a change in your beliefs improved your life?

43. What is something you believe that most people don't?

44. How do you handle it when someone disagrees with something fundamental to your beliefs?

45. What do you believe is the greatest virtue someone can have?

46. How has a particular belief held you back, and how have you overcome it?

47. What does loyalty mean to you, and how has it played a role in your relationships?

48. What personal sacrifices have you made for your beliefs?

49. How do your values guide your consumption or economic choices?

50. What role does gratitude play in your life?

51. How have your beliefs shaped your political views?

52. What is one thing you do regularly that reflects your deepest values?

53. What belief of yours helps you in times of crisis?

54. How do you approach teaching values to others?

55. What is one global issue that deeply concerns you, and why?

56. How do you deal with situations where your values are in conflict?

57. What is a taboo or sensitive topic you believe needs more open discussion?

58. How do you ensure your actions align with your beliefs?

59. What do you think is the key to understanding different viewpoints?

60. How do you maintain your convictions in the face of opposition?

DREAMS AND ASPIRATIONS QUESTIONS

1. What is one dream you have yet to accomplish?

2. How do you envision your life five years from now?

3. What is the biggest dream you've given up on, and why?

4. If you could achieve only one thing in the rest of your life, what would it be?

5. What was your childhood dream job, and how has your perspective on it changed?

6. Who in your life inspires you to pursue your dreams?

7. What do you aspire to be remembered for?

8. Describe a goal you recently set for yourself.

9. How do you deal with setbacks when pursuing your dreams?

10. What skills do you wish to gain that would help you achieve your dreams?

11. If money were no object, what would you spend your life doing?

12. What do you hope to achieve by the end of this year?
13. What is the most ambitious goal you've set for yourself?
14. How do you balance your aspirations with your responsibilities?
15. What personal achievement are you most proud of?
16. How do your dreams influence your daily actions?
17. What do you fear the most when thinking about your future?
18. If you could start over, what dream would you pursue?
19. What steps are you taking to achieve your current aspirations?
20. What dream do you think about the most during your day?
21. How has your definition of success changed over your lifetime?
22. What major change would you make in your life today if you could?
23. Who do you look up to as a role model for success?
24. What is a passion you haven't pursued yet?
25. What legacy do you want to leave behind?
26. How do you motivate yourself when you feel discouraged?
27. What is one unrealistic aspiration you secretly hold?
28. What would you do if you knew you couldn't fail?
29. How do your aspirations align with your current lifestyle?
30. What is the most significant barrier to achieving your dreams?
31. If you could master one skill overnight, what would it be?
32. How does your family influence your aspirations?
33. What is something you're dying to try but haven't had the chance to yet?
34. How do you prioritize your dreams?
35. What dream have you accomplished that you once thought impossible?
36. Who would you ask for help if you were in trouble with achieving a dream?
37. What does personal growth mean to you?
38. What sacrifices have you made to pursue your dreams?
39. What is one dream you've kept secret from everyone?
40. How do societal expectations shape your aspirations?
41. If you could live anywhere in the world, where would it be, and why?
42. What are you most excited about in your future?
43. How do you plan to make the world a better place?
44. What would you study if you went back to school?
45. If you could switch careers right now, what would you choose?
46. What is the biggest risk you're considering taking?
47. How do you prepare for major steps toward your goals?
48. What piece of advice would you give someone who has lost hope in their dreams?
49. How has a significant other influenced your aspirations?
50. What is the most extreme thing you would do to fulfill a dream?
51. How do you record and track your progress towards your goals?
52. How do you celebrate achievements, both big and small?
53. What part of your current lifestyle would you never change, even for your dreams?

54. What is the difference between a dream and a goal for you?

55. If you had to teach something, what would you teach?

56. What would your ideal retirement look like?

57. How do you handle criticism of your aspirations?

58. What part of your dreams do you think are most attainable?

59. How do your dreams affect your relationships with others?

60. What question about your future are you afraid to answer?

RELATIONSHIPS AND SOCIAL LIFE QUESTIONS

1. Who has had the largest impact on your life?

2. Describe your earliest memory of friendship.

3. What qualities do you value most in your friends?

4. Have you ever lost a friend? What happened and how did it affect you?

5. What is your most cherished memory of a family member?

6. How do you handle conflicts in relationships?

7. What is the biggest lesson you've learned from a past relationship?

8. Who is the easiest person for you to talk to and why?

9. How has your relationship with your parents changed over time?

10. What does loyalty mean to you in friendship?

11. Describe when a stranger became a friend.

12. What role do you typically play in your social circles?

13. How do you maintain long-distance relationships?

14. What friendship are you most grateful for?

15. Have you ever had to end a friendship? If so, why?

16. What traits do you admire among your closest friends?

17. How do you show appreciation to others?

18. What was the most meaningful conversation you've had recently?

19. How do you reconnect with someone you've drifted away from?

20. What is the hardest part about relationships with you?

21. Who in your life understands you the best?

22. Describe a time when a friend helped you through a difficult situation.

23. How have your relationships shaped your view of the world?

24. What advice would you give to someone struggling with making friends?

25. How do you balance personal space with closeness in your relationships?

26. What was a significant turning point in a close relationship?

27. How do you deal with jealousy in friendships?

28. What is the most important thing you've done for a friend?

29. How has a friend influenced your life for the better?

30. What do you contribute to your friendships?

31. How do you handle misunderstandings with friends?

32. Describe a time when you felt betrayed by someone you trust.
33. How do you build trust in a relationship?
34. What is something you only share with close friends?
35. What do you expect from your friends in times of need?
36. How do you celebrate your friendships?
37. What is a common challenge you face in your social life?
38. How has your approach to relationships changed as you've aged?
39. Describe a time when a friend changed your opinion about an important issue.
40. What kind of friend are you: listener, advisor, comedian, or motivator?
41. How do you decide whom to trust with your deepest fears?
42. Describe a friendship you admire and why.
43. What makes you feel connected to someone?
44. How do you approach differences in opinion with friends?
45. What lesson from a past relationship do you still think about?
46. How do you support a friend during tough times?
47. How do you handle being the one who always initiates contact in a relationship?
48. What is the most surprising thing you've learned about yourself through your relationships?
49. How important are your family traditions to you and why?
50. Describe a relationship that taught you forgiveness.
51. How has a significant other impacted your beliefs or habits?
52. What is something you need to apologize for to someone?
53. How do you feel about your current social life?
54. What friendship has lasted the longest and what has made it last?
55. Describe a time when you felt completely accepted by others.
56. How do you deal with rejection or exclusion?
57. What aspect of your social life brings you the most joy?
58. What do you do when you feel lonely?
59. How has your role in your family evolved over the years?
60. What is one way you've changed based on feedback from someone close to you?

CAREER AND EDUCATION QUESTIONS

1. What was your first job and what did it teach you about work?
2. Describe a mentor who influenced your career path.
3. What skills from your education do you use in your job today?
4. Have you ever turned a hobby into a profession? How did it go?
5. What is one career you could see yourself in if qualifications and training were not an issue?
6. What professional achievement are you most proud of?
7. Describe a time when you felt underappreciated at work.
8. What subjects were you best at in school, and how have they shaped your career?
9. If you had to teach a class on one topic, what would it be?

10. What does your ideal work environment look like?

11. How do you handle work-related stress?

12. What was the toughest feedback you ever received, and how did you respond?

13. What are your long-term career goals?

14. How important is your work in relation to your overall happiness?

15. What is one thing you wish you had learned earlier in your career?

16. How has your career affected your personal life?

17. What qualities do you admire in your coworkers or employees?

18. How do you stay motivated in your career?

19. Describe a significant professional failure and what you learned from it.

20. What industry changes are you most excited about?

21. How do you balance professional commitments with your personal life?

22. What was the best piece of advice you've received regarding your career?

23. How do you approach networking in your industry?

24. What was a pivotal moment in your education?

25. How do you continue to learn and grow professionally?

26. Describe a job you would never want to have.

27. What challenges are you currently facing at work?

28. What does success in your career look like to you?

29. Have you ever made a dramatic career change? How did it turn out?

30. What are the most important lessons you've learned in your professional life?

31. Who in your field do you most admire and why?

32. What was your favorite part of your education?

33. How do you define a good leader?

34. What career advice would you give to someone just starting out?

35. What are some ethical considerations in your profession?

36. How has mentorship played a role in your career development?

37. Describe an instance where you had to use critical thinking at work.

38. What is the biggest risk you've taken in your career?

39. How do you prepare for a big presentation or meeting?

40. What do you consider your biggest professional mistake?

41. How do you handle disagreements with colleagues?

42. What trends do you predict will shape the future of your industry?

43. How has your approach to your career changed over time?

44. What was your most memorable project or assignment?

45. How do you prioritize tasks on a busy day?

46. What role does teamwork play in your profession?

47. What do you think is the key to maintaining a work-life balance?

48. How do you approach making hard decisions in the workplace?

49. What are you currently trying to improve about yourself professionally?

50. Describe a professional relationship that taught you valuable lessons.

51. What job responsibilities do you find most challenging?

52. What do you wish people understood about your job?
53. What project have you worked on that you are proud of?
54. How do you handle criticism at work?
55. What do you think will be your next big achievement in your career?
56. How do you stay updated with industry trends and knowledge?
57. What part of your job do you find most fulfilling?
58. Have you ever had to compromise your values for your job? How did you handle it?
59. What role does creativity play in your career?
60. What would you consider being your dream job, and why?

HOBBIES AND INTERESTS QUESTIONS

1. What hobby did you pick up early in life and still enjoy?
2. Describe a new hobby you'd like to explore and why.
3. How has your primary hobby influenced your life and choices?
4. What is one hobby that you've given up, and why did you stop?
5. How do you find time for your hobbies with a busy schedule?
6. What is the most unusual hobby you have or would like to have?
7. How do you balance cost and enjoyment in your hobbies?
8. Which hobby brings you the most joy and why?
9. What is a hobby that you and your friends enjoy together?
10. How has a hobby unexpectedly impacted your career or education?
11. What hobby challenges you the most?
12. Describe the last project you completed that's related to your hobby.
13. What hobby have you always wanted to try but haven't yet? What's stopping you?
14. How do your hobbies help you relax and relax?
15. What hobby-related skill are you most proud of developing?
16. Who introduced you to your favorite hobby, and what does that mean to you?
17. What's the most money you've ever spent on a hobby and was it worth it?
18. How do you share your hobbies with others?
19. Which hobby would you turn into a career if you could?
20. What is the most adventurous activity you've undertaken?
21. Do you prefer hobbies you can do alone or with others? Why?
22. How has technology affected your hobbies?
23. What is the biggest challenge you've faced in your favorite hobby?
24. How do you discover new hobbies or interests?
25. What is the best way to introduce others to your hobbies?
26. What hobby do you think you'd be good at, and why haven't you started?
27. How do hobbies influence your social interactions?
28. What is your favorite thing to create, make, or build?
29. Have you ever took part in a competition related to your hobby? What was that experience like?

30. What hobby has been the most rewarding to learn and why?
31. How do you measure progress in your hobbies?
32. What has been your most significant failure in a hobby, and what did you learn from it?
33. How do your hobbies reflect your personality?
34. Do you have any hobbies that are unusual or unique?
35. How do you stay motivated when progress in a hobby is slow?
36. What resources do you use to improve your skills in your hobbies?
37. How has your approach to hobbies changed as you've gotten older?
38. What hobby would you recommend to everyone and why?
39. How do your hobbies help you connect with your cultural or family heritage?
40. What is one hobby that helps you feel more connected to nature?
41. Have any of your hobbies developed into passions? Describe that evolution.
42. How do you manage to prioritize your hobbies when you have limited time?
43. What's the most important lesson you've learned through your hobbies?
44. Have you ever taught a hobby to someone else? Describe that experience.
45. What is your favorite tool or piece of equipment for your hobbies and why?
46. How do your hobbies influence your mental and physical health?
47. Describe a memorable experience related to one of your hobbies.
48. What hobby helps you escape the stress of everyday life?
49. How has engaging in hobbies improved your life?
50. What is the most creative hobby you've attempted?
51. How do you incorporate your hobbies into your daily routine?
52. What is the community like around one of your hobbies?
53. Have you ever had to give up a hobby because of physical limitations? What was that like?
54. How do you stay informed and updated about new trends in your hobbies?
55. What is the most fulfilling aspect of engaging in hobbies for you?
56. Have your hobbies ever brought you into contact with people from different backgrounds? Describe that interaction.
57. What hobby-related goal are you currently working towards?
58. How do your hobbies influence the way you decorate or maintain your living space?
59. What has been your most significant investment in a hobby?
60. Describe a hobby that you lost interest in and why.

TRAVEL AND ADVENTURE QUESTIONS

1. What is the most memorable trip you have ever taken?
2. Describe a place you visited that felt like a different world.
3. What is the furthest you've ever traveled from home?
4. Which travel experience exceeded your expectations the most?
5. What is one place you would love to visit again? Why?
6. How has traveling changed your perspective on life?

7. What is the most adventurous thing you've ever done?

8. Which country's culture fascinates you the most?

9. What was your biggest culture shock while traveling?

10. Have you ever traveled alone? Describe that experience.

11. What is your favorite way to travel: plane, boat, car, or train?

12. What are the three items you can't travel without?

13. Describe a time when something went wrong on a trip.

14. What is the most beautiful natural wonder you have visited?

15. What city in the world would you choose to live in for a year?

16. How do you prepare for a trip to a new place?

17. What's the best meal you've had while traveling?

18. What languages have you learned or wish to learn for travel?

19. What's the most unusual mode of transportation you've tried?

20. How do you keep memories from your travels?

21. Describe a person you met while traveling who affected you.

22. What travel tradition do you have?

23. What is the most surprising thing you've learned through travel?

24. What is your favorite type of landscape to explore?

25. How do you choose your travel destinations?

26. What was the most impromptu trip you've taken?

27. How do you deal with language barriers?

28. What's the best travel advice you've ever received?

29. Describe a historical site that left a powerful impression on you.

30. What's the most peaceful place you've visited?

31. How do you make the most out of a quick trip?

32. What souvenirs do you collect from your travels?

33. What is the scariest experience you've had while traveling?

34. How has travel strengthened your relationships?

35. What travel mishap makes you laugh now?

36. What's your strategy for overcoming jet lag?

37. Describe a wildlife encounter you had while traveling.

38. What is the most interesting museum you've visited?

39. How do you respect local customs and traditions while traveling?

40. What do you always do on the first day of a trip?

41. What's the longest road trip you've ever been on?

42. How do you stay healthy while traveling?

43. What's a travel myth you've debunked from your own experience?

44. What was your most relaxing vacation?

45. Describe the best shop or market you've visited abroad.

46. How do you decide what activities to do while traveling?

47. What is the most challenging hike or physical activity you've done on a trip?

48. How do you handle homesickness when traveling?

49. What's your favorite travel memory with friends or family?
50. What piece of art have you seen while traveling that moved you?
51. How do you approach eating local foods in new places?
52. What's a travel habit you've developed?
53. How do you budget for your travels?
54. What's the most spontaneous adventure you've embarked on?
55. How do you document your travels?
56. What's the best travel lesson you've learned from someone else?
57. How do you choose travel companions?
58. What destination have you found to be overrated?
59. What's one travel experience that has taught you about resilience?
60. How do travel and adventure influence your life at home?

HEALTH AND WELLBEING QUESTIONS

1. What does good health mean to you?
2. How do you balance physical and mental health?
3. What are your key habits for maintaining your health?
4. Describe a time when your health significantly impacted your life.
5. How has your approach to health changed over the years?
6. What's the most important health lesson you've learned from your family?
7. What activities do you find most beneficial for your mental health?
8. What motivates you to stay active and healthy?
9. How do you manage stress on a tough day?
10. What are your strategies for dealing with insomnia or sleep issues?
11. What dietary habits do you believe have the biggest impact on your health?
12. Describe a health scare and how it changed your perspective on life.
13. What's your approach to holistic health practices?
14. How often do you prioritize self-care and what does that look like for you?
15. What's the hardest part about maintaining a healthy lifestyle?
16. How do you incorporate physical activity into your daily routine?
17. What mental health resource has been most helpful to you?
18. How do you handle setbacks in your health or fitness goals?
19. What have you learned about your health by observing your parents or older relatives?
20. How do you decide which health information to trust?
21. What is your opinion on the balance between traditional medicine and alternative treatments?
22. How has your understanding of nutrition developed?
23. What's one healthy habit you wish everyone would adopt?
24. Describe a wellness trend you tried and how it turned out for you.
25. How do you measure the success of your health regimen?
26. What role does genetics play in your approach to health and wellness?

27. How do you stay motivated when healthy improvements are slow?
28. What is your favorite form of exercise and why?
29. How do you manage health advice from non-professionals?
30. What is your biggest challenge for eating healthy?
31. How has a friend or partner influenced your health habits?
32. What's the most unexpected benefit you've experienced from improving your health?
33. How do you find time for regular medical check-ups and health screenings?
34. What's your approach to mental wellness during the winter?
35. How do you recharge on a physically or emotionally draining day?
36. What changes in your body have you noticed as you've gotten older?
37. How do you handle differing health opinions in your family?
38. What's a common health myth you used to believe?
39. How does technology affect your health and wellbeing?
40. What's the best health advice you've ever received?
41. How do you support friends or family members in their health journeys?
42. Describe a positive health habit you've developed in the last year.
43. How has your health influenced your career choices?
44. What's the most impactful health book or article you've read?
45. How do you balance health commitments with your social life?
46. What's the most challenging outdoor activity you've tried?
47. How has your sleep pattern changed with age?
48. What health aspect are you currently focusing on improving?
49. How do you deal with anxiety or depression?
50. What's your strategy for staying hydrated throughout the day?
51. How has your fitness routine changed over time?
52. What role does community or social support play in your wellbeing?
53. What's your biggest health-related fear?
54. How do you educate yourself about health and wellness?
55. What impact has quitting a bad habit had on your health?
56. How do you handle health-related setbacks or relapses?
57. What's your perspective on aging and health?
58. How do personal beliefs align with your health practices?
59. What's the longest you've gone without sleep and why?
60. How do you use technology to improve your health?

FAVORITES AND PREFERENCES QUESTIONS

1. What is your favorite book and what impact did it have on you?
2. Describe your favorite childhood memory.
3. What is your favorite way to spend a rainy day?
4. Who is your favorite author and why?

5. What is your favorite holiday and how do you like to celebrate it?

6. What song do you never get tired of listening to?

7. What is your favorite meal to cook and why?

8. Who was your favorite teacher and what did they teach you?

9. What is your favorite quote and how has it influenced you?

10. Describe your favorite place in the world.

11. What is your favorite family tradition?

12. What is your favorite movie and why does it stand out to you?

13. What is your favorite thing to do to relax?

14. What is your favorite season and what do you like most about it?

15. Who is your favorite artist (painter, musician, writer, etc.) and what draws you to their work?

16. What is your favorite memory of your best friend?

17. What is your favorite type of weather and why?

18. Describe your favorite piece of clothing.

19. What is your favorite animal, and have you ever seen one in the wild?

20. What is your favorite sport to watch or play?

21. What is your favorite hobby or pastime?

22. What is your favorite type of cuisine?

23. Who is your favorite fictional character?

24. What is your favorite app on your phone and why?

25. What is your favorite game to play (video, board, or sport)?

26. What is your favorite local restaurant and what do you order there?

27. What is your favorite workout or physical activity?

28. What is your favorite way to spend time outdoors?

29. What is your favorite memory of your parents?

30. What is your favorite aspect of your job or career?

31. What is your favorite thing about yourself?

32. What is your favorite time of day and why?

33. Describe your favorite piece of art in your home.

34. What was your favorite subject in school and how has it shaped you?

35. What is your favorite thing to do on weekends?

36. What is your favorite comfort food?

37. What is your favorite podcast or radio show?

38. What is your favorite place to shop and what do you buy there?

39. What is your favorite plant or flower?

40. What is your favorite type of dessert?

41. What is your favorite scent or smell?

42. What is your favorite way to travel (car, plane, bike, etc.)?

43. What is your favorite childhood toy and do you still have it?

44. What is your favorite piece of technology and how has it improved your life?

45. What is your favorite age you've been so far and why?

46. What is your favorite cultural activity to take part in or observe?

47. What is your favorite thing to do with your family?
48. What is your favorite memory from high school?
49. What is your favorite kind of music to listen to?
50. What is your favorite photograph you've taken?
51. What is your favorite holiday decoration?
52. What is your favorite way to express creativity?
53. What is your favorite piece of advice you've received?
54. What is your favorite type of bird?
55. What is your favorite memory of your grandparents?
56. What is your favorite thing to do for others?
57. What is your favorite myth or legend?
58. What is your favorite childhood game?
59. What is your favorite way to celebrate achievements?
60. What is your favorite way to unwind after a long day?

TECHNOLOGY AND MEDIA QUESTIONS

1. What was the first piece of technology you owned, and how did it impact you?
2. How do you think social media has changed your relationships?
3. What app do you use most often, and why?
4. Describe your ideal technology-free day.
5. What piece of outdated technology do you miss and why?
6. How do you stay informed about current events and which sources do you trust?
7. What is your opinion on the impact of video games on society?
8. How has technology improved your work or personal life?
9. What concerns do you have about the future of technology?
10. How do you balance your online and offline life?
11. What movie or TV show do you think accurately depicts our future with technology?
12. What role does technology play in your education or learning?
13. Do you prefer eBooks or physical books, and why?
14. How do you protect your privacy online?
15. What is one piece of technology you couldn't live without?
16. How do you decide what media content is appropriate for you or your family?
17. What technological advancement are you most excited about?
18. How has technology helped you connect with others?
19. What is the most recent gadget you purchased, and has it lived up to your expectations?
20. How do you detox from digital media?
21. What is your favorite video game, and what makes it special to you?
22. How has technology affected your attention span or reading habits?
23. What is your go-to app for relaxation or mindfulness?
24. How do you think virtual reality will change entertainment?

25. What is the most valuable thing you have learned from a podcast?
26. How do you approach social media: as a creator, consumer, or both?
27. What are your thoughts on artificial intelligence in everyday life?
28. How do you ensure your security and privacy when using new technology?
29. What old school technology do you think should make a comeback?
30. How do you use technology to stay organized?
31. What's your stance on the use of drones in civilian life?
32. How do you feel about the ethical implications of biotechnology?
33. What is the most unexpected way you've seen technology impact someone's life?
34. How do you think technology has changed learning for the younger generation?
35. What tech gadget is on your wish list and why?
36. What is your favorite form of digital entertainment (streaming, gaming, social media) and why?
37. How do you think dependency on technology affects mental health?
38. What steps do you take to reduce screen time?
39. What was the last online video that made you laugh?
40. How do you think the internet has changed the concept of community?
41. What science fiction technology do you wish existed today?
42. How do you navigate the overwhelming amount of information available online?
43. What do you think about the quality of journalism in the digital age?
44. How has the music industry changed with technology?
45. What is the most interesting documentary you've watched that technology influenced?
46. How do you feel about the pace of technological changes today?
47. What role does technology play in your fitness or health regimen?
48. How has technology influenced your shopping habits?
49. What's the biggest drawback of the digital age for you?
50. How do you use technology to foster creativity?
51. What is the most interesting online community you are part of?
52. How has digital photography changed your approach to memories?
53. What are your rules for using technology in social settings?
54. How has technology influenced your travel experiences?
55. What online resource has significantly influenced your education or self-development?
56. How do you feel about the permanence of digital footprints?
57. What are your thoughts on the digital divide and access to technology?
58. How do you think technology has changed parenting?
59. What online trend do you find most puzzling?
60. How do you see the role of technology evolving in your life?

SELF-HELP AND PERSONAL DEVELOPMENT QUESTIONS

1. What is one self-help book that has profoundly affected your life?
2. What personal development goal are you currently working towards?

3. How do you handle criticism and use it for your growth?
4. What is a fear you have overcome, and how did you do it?
5. Describe a time when you had to adapt to a significant change.
6. What are your key strategies for managing stress?
7. What habit would you most like to break, and why?
8. What is one thing you do regularly that helps boost your self-esteem?
9. Who do you turn to for advice when you're struggling?
10. What does personal growth mean to you?
11. What is one life skill you wish someone had taught you as a child?
12. How do you stay motivated when progress seems slow?
13. Describe a moment when you felt genuine pride in yourself.
14. What is the biggest obstacle you've faced in your personal development?
15. How has your understanding of yourself changed in the last five years?
16. What steps do you take when you feel overwhelmed?
17. What role does gratitude play in your life?
18. How do you cultivate patience in challenging situations?
19. What small victory have you achieved recently?
20. What does success look like to you outside of professional achievements?
21. How do you maintain focus on long-term goals?
22. What personal strengths have you relied on most in your life?
23. How do you approach setting new goals for yourself?
24. What is a lesson you've learned from a past failure?
25. How do you balance ambition with contentment?
26. What is a quote that inspires you regularly?
27. Describe a habit you've developed that has positively influenced your life.
28. What do you consider your greatest personal achievement?
29. How do you recharge after a hard day?
30. What practices help you maintain mental health?
31. How do you find a balance between work, home, and personal time?
32. What is the most important value you live by?
33. How do you practice self-compassion?
34. What is the toughest feedback you've ever received and how did you respond?
35. What is something new you've learned about yourself this year?
36. How do you help others in their personal development?
37. What is one area of your life where you feel stuck?
38. How has your perspective on what's important in life changed over time?
39. What book or resource do you recommend for personal growth?
40. How do you handle moments of self-doubt?
41. What is an aspect of your personality that you've worked hard to improve?
42. How do you prioritize your personal well-being?
43. What activity makes you feel like your best self?
44. Describe a challenge you're facing right now and your plan to overcome it.

45. What personal traits do you admire in others and strive to develop in yourself?

46. How do you celebrate your accomplishments?

47. What does being "mindful" mean to you, and how do you practice it?

48. How do you stay true to your values when pressured by others?

49. What is one piece of advice you would give someone trying to overcome a hardship?

50. How do you manage the balance between giving and receiving in your relationships?

51. What are you most grateful for in your personal development journey?

52. What is a change you made in your life that has led to significant growth?

53. How do you handle setbacks and roadblocks in your personal growth?

54. What does resilience mean to you, and can you give an example of when you had to be resilient?

55. What personal sacrifice have you made that led to unexpected personal growth?

56. How do you measure personal success, and has this changed over time?

57. What life lessons do you wish to pass on to others?

58. How do you incorporate learning from others into your personal growth?

59. What is a daily or weekly ritual that contributes to your personal development?

60. How do you maintain enthusiasm for life's journey?

EDUCATION AND LEARNING QUESTIONS

1. What was your favorite subject in school and why?

2. Describe a teacher who had a significant impact on your life.

3. What is one thing you wish schools had taught?

4. How do you prefer to learn new skills—through books, videos, hands-on experience, or lectures?

5. What educational challenge have you overcome?

6. What is the most valuable lesson you learned from your education?

7. How has your approach to learning changed as you've aged?

8. What subject do you wish you had paid more attention to in school?

9. What is the last book you read that taught you something unexpected?

10. How do you incorporate continuous learning into your daily routine?

11. Describe an educational experience that changed your perspective.

12. What do you think is missing from today's educational system?

13. How do you tackle learning something outside your comfort zone?

14. What role has formal or informal education played in your career?

15. What is a skill you've learned that you never thought you would?

16. Who is your learning role model, and why?

17. What is a recent educational trend you find interesting or valuable?

18. What is the most challenging educational material you have tackled?

19. How do you motivate yourself to keep learning?

20. What do you consider your most significant learning achievement?

21. What educational resource do you find most effective?

22. How has online education influenced your learning habits?
23. What foreign language would you like to learn and why?
24. What educational goal are you currently working towards?
25. How do you apply what you learn in your personal or professional life?
26. What is your opinion of lifelong learning?
27. What is one thing you learned later in life that you wish you had learned earlier?
28. How do you handle learning from failure?
29. What learning method works best for you?
30. Describe a time when learning something new had a direct impact on your life.
31. What historical period or event do you wish you knew more about?
32. What book significantly shaped your way of thinking?
33. How do you deal with educational setbacks?
34. What is the most interesting documentary you've ever watched?
35. How do you assess the credibility of an educational source?
36. What is one area of your professional field you want to learn more about?
37. How has your education affected your worldview?
38. What is a common misconception about your field of study?
39. What motivates you to learn about new topics?
40. How do you balance practical and theoretical learning?
41. What piece of advice would you give someone starting their educational journey?
42. What was your biggest takeaway from your highest level of formal education?
43. How do you make learning fun for yourself or others?
44. What is the biggest challenge the education system faces today?
45. How do you use technology to enhance your learning?
46. Which subject do you think the education system undervalues?
47. How do you engage with new and challenging ideas?
48. What role does collaboration play in your learning process?
49. How has a mentor or coach influenced your educational journey?
50. What is the most important skill you've learned on your own?
51. How do you prioritize your learning projects or goals?
52. Describe an instance where interdisciplinary learning opened new doors for you.
53. What is your strategy for retaining information?
54. How do you take advantage of educational opportunities?
55. What is one educational experience you believe everyone should have?
56. How do you challenge the limits of your knowledge?
57. What learning experience has made you a better person?
58. How do you react when you find learning difficult or frustrating?
59. What is the most inspiring educational story you've heard?
60. How do you measure the success of your learning experiences?

CREATIVITY AND INNOVATION QUESTIONS

1. What does creativity mean to you?
2. Describe the last time you felt truly inspired.
3. What barriers do you face when trying to be creative?
4. How do you overcome a creative block?
5. Can you name a project that was a turning point in your understanding of creativity?
6. How do you cultivate new ideas?
7. What environment stimulates your creativity the most?
8. How do you incorporate innovation into your daily tasks?
9. Who is your creative role model, and why?
10. What innovation in the last decade has most impressed you?
11. Describe an instance where a creative approach solved a problem for you.
12. How do you balance tradition with innovation in your work or life?
13. What is the most unconventional idea you have pursued?
14. How do you react to criticism of your creative ideas?
15. What project are you working on that excites you?
16. How does technology enhance your creativity?
17. In what ways do you share your creativity with others?
18. What creative skill would you like to learn or improve?
19. How has your creativity developed over the years?
20. What artistic medium have you always wanted to explore?
21. How do you find inspiration when it feels lacking?
22. Describe a risk you took that had a creative payoff.
23. What is the most creative aspect of your personality?
24. How do you push the boundaries of your creativity?
25. How does your cultural background influence your creative expressions?
26. What is the biggest creative challenge you've faced?
27. How do you integrate creativity into your routine?
28. Describe a piece of art that changed your perspective.
29. What book has significantly influenced your creative thinking?
30. How do you collaborate creatively with others?
31. What does innovation look like in your field of work?
32. How do you nurture creative thinking in stressful situations?
33. What are your thoughts on the future of creativity in technology?
34. How travels affect your creativity?
35. What project have you done that you believe was truly innovative?
36. How do you react when others reject your creative ideas?
37. What role does intuition play in your creative process?
38. How do you prioritize your creative projects?
39. Describe how you would teach creativity to someone else.

40. What misconception about being creative would you like to change?

41. How do you maintain your originality in a world of constant innovation?

42. Describe an innovation you think the world needs urgently.

43. How do you balance creativity with practicality?

44. What is the most creative solution you've seen in a common problem?

45. How does nature influence your creative outputs?

46. What music enhances your creativity?

47. How do you document or track your creative ideas?

48. What is the strangest source of inspiration you have encountered?

49. How does being creative make you feel?

50. What role does feedback play in your creative process?

51. Describe a time when creativity helped you in your personal life.

52. What are your favorite tools for creating?

53. How do you recharge your creative energy?

54. What is the relationship between creativity and innovation in your view?

55. Describe how you handled a failure in a creative project.

56. How do you stay committed to a long-term creative project?

57. How do you manage the balance between new ideas and finishing projects?

58. What future creative project are you most excited about?

59. How do you use creativity to improve everyday tasks?

60. What would you say to someone who thinks they are not creative?

FINANCIAL ATTITUDES QUESTIONS

1. How do you define financial success?

2. What is your earliest memory related to money?

3. How has your upbringing influenced your financial habits?

4. What is one financial goal you are currently working towards?

5. How do you approach budgeting and financial planning?

6. What's the most challenging financial decision you've ever made?

7. What does financial freedom mean to you?

8. How do you prioritize your spending?

9. What financial risks are you willing to take?

10. How do you manage financial stress?

11. What's the best financial advice you've ever received?

12. How do you approach saving for retirement?

13. What's one financial mistake you wish you could redo?

14. How do you educate yourself about finances?

15. What impact has money had on your personal relationships?

16. How do you balance spending on yourself versus saving for the future?

17. What's the most extravagant purchase you've ever made, and do you regret it?

18. How do you approach investments and diversifying your portfolio?

19. What's your strategy for dealing with unexpected expenses?

20. How do you feel about debt and borrowing money?

21. What lessons have you learned from your financial experiences?

22. How has your financial situation influenced your lifestyle choices?

23. What financial habits are you trying to improve?

24. How do you approach discussions about money within your family or with your partner?

25. What's the biggest financial risk you've ever taken?

26. How do you decide what's worth spending money on?

27. What role does money play in your sense of security?

28. How do you feel about lending money to friends or family?

29. What's your approach to charitable giving and philanthropy?

30. How has your career affected your financial outlook?

31. What financial trends or news do you follow?

32. How do you plan for major life expenses (e.g., education, housing, health care)?

33. How do you manage your mental and emotional health concerning financial issues?

34. What's the most valuable thing you've ever bought?

35. How do you react to financial setbacks?

36. What are your financial red flags when planning your budget?

37. How do you decide when to splurge and when to save?

38. How has your financial confidence changed over time?

39. What tools or resources do you use to manage your finances?

40. What's the best investment you've ever made?

41. How do you approach financial discussions with your children or younger family members?

42. How do you feel about your current financial situation?

43. What are your long-term financial aspirations?

44. How do you measure financial success in your personal and professional life?

45. What steps are you taking to secure your financial future?

46. How do you prepare financially for major life changes?

47. What financial sacrifices have you made to achieve your goals?

48. How do you approach money management in your household?

49. What's the biggest financial lesson you've learned so far?

50. How do you feel about money and happiness?

51. How has your approach to money changed with age?

52. What are your strategies for increasing your income?

53. How do you manage loans and credit?

54. What's your perspective on wealth and social responsibility?

55. How transparent are you about your finances with others?

56. What's one financial habit you'd like to pass on to others?

57. How do you balance risk and security in your financial decisions?

58. What are your concerns about your financial future?

59. How do you respond to financial advice from others?

60. What financial legacy do you hope to leave?

CULTURAL HERITAGE QUESTIONS

1. What aspects of your cultural heritage are you most proud of?
2. How do you celebrate the traditional holidays of your culture?
3. What traditional foods from your culture do you most enjoy?
4. How has your cultural background influenced your beliefs and values?
5. Can you speak any languages that are part of your cultural heritage?
6. What cultural traditions do you continue to practice?
7. How do you keep your culture alive if you are living in a different country?
8. What stories from your elders have impacted you the most?
9. How does your culture influence your daily life?
10. What is one cultural stereotype that you want to correct?
11. How do you educate others about your culture?
12. What cultural skill or craft have you learned from your family?
13. How has your understanding of your cultural heritage changed as you've aged?
14. What traditional music or dance from your culture do you like most?
15. How do you feel when you meet someone from the same cultural background?
16. What aspects of your culture do you find challenging?
17. How do you reconcile differences between your cultural identity and the culture where you live?
18. What cultural festival have you always wanted to attend?
19. How does your family keep its cultural heritage alive?
20. What cultural figure has significantly influenced you?
21. Have you visited the country or countries of your ancestors? Describe that experience.
22. What part of your cultural heritage do you wish you knew more about?
23. How do you pass on your cultural traditions to younger generations?
24. What is the most important lesson you've learned from your cultural background?
25. What cultural customs do you find most meaningful?
26. How has cultural heritage shaped your career choices?
27. What cultural heritage sites are you most interested in visiting?
28. How do different generations in your family view cultural heritage?
29. How do you incorporate traditional dress into your life, if at all?
30. What is your favorite piece of folklore or legend from your culture?
31. How does your culture influence your relationships?
32. What traditional art forms from your culture do you most appreciate?
33. How has globalization affected your perception of cultural identity?
34. What misconceptions do people often have about your culture?
35. How do you manage the preservation of cultural identity?
36. What cultural rituals do you find most fascinating?
37. How does your cultural background influence your approach to parenting?

38. What traditional methods of healing from your culture do you practice or believe in?

39. How do you balance modern life with traditional values?

40. What historical event within your culture has had a significant impact on you?

41. How does language play a role in preserving your cultural identity?

42. What is one cultural item that holds significant meaning for you?

43. How do you celebrate milestones according to your cultural traditions?

44. What traditional games or sports from your culture do you play?

45. How has your cultural heritage influenced your spiritual beliefs?

46. What cultural taboos or superstitions were you taught?

47. How do you feel about the commercialization of certain aspects of your culture?

48. What traditional practices from your culture do you find difficult to explain to others?

49. How has your perspective on your cultural heritage evolved over time?

50. What role does community play in your cultural expressions?

51. How do you respond to cultural appropriation when you see it?

52. What aspect of your culture brings you the most joy?

53. How do you handle conflicting cultural values when interacting with others?

54. What does cultural pride mean to you?

55. How does your cultural background influence your sense of identity?

56. What traditional story or myth do you feel everyone should know about?

57. How does your culture approach the concept of respect and honor?

58. What are the benefits and challenges of a multicultural society from your perspective?

59. How do you see the future of your cultural traditions?

60. What message would you like to pass on about your culture to the wider world?

LIFE MILESTONES QUESTIONS

1. What was your proudest moment and why?

2. Describe the day you felt you became an adult.

3. What was your biggest achievement in school?

4. Recall your graduation day. What emotions did you feel?

5. What has been the most significant birthday of your life so far?

6. Describe the moment you first fell in love.

7. What is the most important lesson you learned from your parents?

8. Reflect on the first job you have ever had. What did it teach you?

9. When did you first experience a major setback, and how did you handle it?

10. What was your first major purchase, and why was it significant?

11. Describe the moment you felt most proud of a family member.

12. What has been your biggest financial milestone?

13. When did you first travel alone, and what did you learn about yourself?

14. Describe the experience of moving out on your own for the first time.

15. When did you feel you truly achieved something extraordinary?

16. Reflect on a time when you overcame a significant fear.
17. What milestone are you most looking forward to?
18. What was a pivotal moment in your career?
19. When did you first feel you made a real impact on someone else's life?
20. What was the most challenging decision you've made in your life?
21. Describe the moment you realized your own strength.
22. When did you first understand the value of friendship?
23. What was your biggest failure, and what did you learn from it?
24. When have you felt the most satisfied with your life?
25. Describe when you forgave someone who deeply hurt you.
26. What was a turning point in your personal development?
27. When did you feel you followed your heart against all odds?
28. What was your most memorable holiday and why?
29. Reflect on the moment you felt you truly understood your purpose.
30. When did you feel most connected to your cultural heritage?
31. Describe a milestone that took you by surprise.
32. What moment in your life would you like to relive?
33. When did you take a significant risk, and what was the outcome?
34. Describe the first time you felt truly independent.
35. When did you realize your own resilience?
36. What was the most difficult ethical decision you've had to make?
37. Describe when you felt a significant spiritual awakening.
38. What event marked a major change in your lifestyle?
39. When did you feel you truly made peace with your past?
40. What was the first major conflict you resolved, and how did you do it?
41. When did you last push yourself beyond what you thought was possible?
42. Reflect on the moment you first experienced a profound sense of joy.
43. What was your most impactful act of kindness?
44. When did you feel you had a significant effect on your community?
45. What was the first major project or task you completed successfully?
46. Describe the moment you felt most connected to nature.
47. When did you last experience a moment of pure contentment?
48. What personal record have you set that makes you proud?
49. When did you last reassess your life goals, and why?
50. What was the moment you felt most challenged intellectually?
51. When have you had to adapt the most to a new situation?
52. Describe a milestone related to your health.
53. What has been the biggest turning point in your relationships?
54. When did you feel most aligned with your values?
55. Reflect on a time when you had to stand up for what you believe in.
56. Describe a moment when you had to let go of someone or something important.
57. When did you feel there was a major shift in your personal philosophy?

58. What was a milestone that significantly shaped your view of the world?

59. Reflect on a time when you chose a path less traveled.

60. Describe when you felt complete closure on an important chapter of your life.

FEARS AND PHOBIAS QUESTIONS

1. What is your greatest fear?

2. How has a specific fear affected your daily life?

3. Can you trace the origin of any of your fears or phobias?

4. What steps have you taken to overcome a significant fear?

5. Describe a time when you confronted a fear head-on.

6. How do you typically react in situations where you feel afraid?

7. What fears have you inherited from your family?

8. Do you believe fears are rational, and why or why not?

9. How do your fears affect your personal relationships?

10. What strategies have been most effective in managing your phobias?

11. Have you ever sought professional help in managing fears or phobias?

12. How do you comfort yourself when you feel scared?

13. What is the smallest fear you've conquered?

14. Describe a fear you had as a child that you no longer have.

15. How do you prepare yourself to face a fearful situation?

16. What fear has taught you the most about yourself?

17. What phobias do you find most intriguing or unusual?

18. How do you distinguish between a rational and an irrational fear?

19. What advice would you give to someone who shares a similar fear as yours?

20. How has facing your fears changed you as a person?

21. Do you feel your fears limit your opportunities?

22. How do societal fears influence your views or behaviors?

23. What methods do you use to calm yourself in the face of fear?

24. Have you ever let go of an opportunity because of fear?

25. What is a common fear that you don't have?

26. How do you talk about your fears with others?

27. What animal are you most afraid of, and why?

28. How has understanding your fears improved your mental health?

29. What fictional character fears can you most relate to?

30. What do you fear most about the future?

31. How has a book or movie influenced your perception of fear?

32. What aspects of your career do you fear?

33. What physical sensations do you experience when you feel afraid?

34. Have your fears changed as you've gotten older?

35. What fear would you most like to conquer this year?

36. How do cultural or family beliefs shape your fears?

37. What do you think your fears say about you?

38. Describe a dream where you faced a fear.

39. How do you help others who are dealing with fears?

40. What are your fears about your physical health?

41. What do you find most frightening about change?

42. How does fear affect your decision-making process?

43. What scares you the most about the idea of failure?

44. How do you manage anxiety related to your fears?

45. What role does the media play in amplifying your fears?

46. How does fear influence your spiritual beliefs?

47. What safety precautions do you take because of fear?

48. What is something you avoid because of fear?

49. How has your greatest fear grown over time?

50. What is the most courageous thing you've done despite being afraid?

51. How does fear affect your educational or learning experiences?

52. What do you fear about losing?

53. How does fear impact your leadership or management style?

54. What does fear prevent you from doing?

55. How do you foresee overcoming your fears in the future?

56. What would you do if you weren't afraid?

57. How does fear affect your creativity?

58. What historical or global fears do you find most impactful?

59. How do you think technology amplifies or eases fears?

60. What fear do you wish more people understood or recognized?

DECISION MAKING QUESTIONS

1. How do you approach making tough decisions?

2. What was the most challenging decision you made this year?

3. How do you weigh the pros and cons when making a choice?

4. Can you describe a time when you decided too quickly?

5. What tools or methods do you use to aid in decision-making?

6. How do you handle decisions that involve significant risk?

7. What is the best decision you've ever made?

8. How do you deal with regret after making a decision?

9. Who do you turn to for advice when facing a tough choice?

10. How much does a potential outcome influence your decision-making?

11. What was a decision that completely changed your life?

12. How do you know when to follow your head versus your heart?

13. Do you often seek second opinions before making important decisions?

14. How has your decision-making process evolved over time?

15. What role does intuition play in your choices?

16. How do you cope with the pressure of decision-making in your professional life?

17. Describe a time when you had to make a decision without all the information you needed.

18. How do you prioritize when multiple decisions need attention?

19. What decision do you keep putting off?

20. How do you handle decisions that affect other people?

21. Can you think of a decision that taught you a valuable lesson?

22. How do you manage the stress of consequential decisions?

23. What is the quickest decision you've ever made that had a significant impact?

24. How do you revisit a decision if you start to second-guess it?

25. What has been your most recent major decision, and how did you come to it?

26. How do you deal with indecision?

27. What factors do you consider most crucial when making a life-changing decision?

28. How do you prepare for decisions that you can expect?

29. Describe a time when your decision had an unexpected outcome.

30. What is the hardest part of decision-making for you?

31. How do you reflect on and evaluate your past decisions?

32. How do you respond when someone challenges or criticizes your decisions?

33. What is the most important decision you've made in your personal life?

34. How do you ensure your decisions align with your long-term goals?

35. How do you handle decisions in emotionally charged situations?

36. What influence does your cultural background have on your decision-making?

37. How do you balance individual desires with family or community needs?

38. What role does fear play in your decision-making process?

39. How do you respond when you make a wrong decision?

40. What strategies do you use to simplify complex decisions?

41. How do you ensure fairness in your decisions?

42. Describe a decision you made that was influenced by peer pressure.

43. How do you decide when to compromise and when to stand firm?

44. What impact do financial considerations have on your decisions?

45. How do you approach ethical dilemmas?

46. How does your decision-making process differ in personal vs. professional contexts?

47. What is a decision you made that felt empowering?

48. How do you handle situations where you must decide under time pressure?

49. What's an example of a small decision that led to a big change?

50. How do you distinguish between multiple good options?

51. How do you recover and move forward from a poor decision?

52. What decisions are you glad you made, despite initial doubts?

53. How do you assess risk in decision-making?

54. What decisions would you like to improve at making?

55. How do you practice making better decisions every day?

56. What role does research play in your decision-making?

57. How has your decision-making impacted your relationships?
58. What have you learned about yourself through your decision-making habits?
59. Describe a decision that involved a major sacrifice.
60. What future decision are you preparing for now?

MINDFULNESS AND SPIRITUALITY QUESTIONS

1. What does spirituality mean to you?
2. How do you practice mindfulness in your daily routine?
3. What spiritual beliefs guide your decisions?
4. Can you describe when you felt a deep connection to the world around you?
5. How has your understanding of spirituality changed over time?
6. What mindfulness exercise has significantly affected your life?
7. How do you find peace in stressful situations?
8. What are your thoughts on the afterlife?
9. How do you cultivate gratitude in your life?
10. What role does meditation play in your spiritual practice?
11. How do you reconnect with yourself when you feel lost?
12. What book on spirituality has influenced you the most?
13. How do you maintain a sense of presence throughout the day?
14. What spiritual tradition fascinates you, and why?
15. Describe a spiritual ritual that you find comforting.
16. How does your spiritual belief influence your relationships with others?
17. What is the most profound spiritual experience you have had?
18. How do you handle doubts about your spiritual beliefs?
19. What does being mindful mean to you in your daily life?
20. How has spirituality helped you cope with a major life event?
21. What questions do you often ponder about the universe?
22. How do you incorporate mindfulness into challenging tasks?
23. What mantra or affirmation do you find most powerful?
24. Describe a moment of mindfulness that gave you a new perspective.
25. What does the concept of karma mean to you?
26. How do you practice compassion towards others?
27. What spiritual figure do you admire most and why?
28. How has mindfulness affected your physical health?
29. What is the biggest challenge you face in your spiritual practice?
30. How do you balance your material desires with spiritual needs?
31. What mindful habit has transformed your daily life the most?
32. How do you approach forgiveness, both giving and receiving?
33. What aspects of nature inspire you spiritually?
34. How do you respond when your spiritual beliefs are challenged?

35. What spiritual or religious ceremonies do you find meaningful?

36. How has mindfulness helped you in your professional life?

37. Describe a practice or technique that helps you stay grounded.

38. What lessons have you learned through meditation?

39. How do you deal with spiritual or existential anxiety?

40. What does the idea of a soul mean to you?

41. How has engaging with different cultures affected your spiritual views?

42. What do you believe is your purpose in life?

43. How do you use mindfulness to enhance your creativity?

44. What does self-awareness mean to you within your spiritual journey?

45. Describe a change in your life that was influenced by spiritual growth.

46. How do you apply spiritual principles in difficult times?

47. What spiritual practice would you like to explore more deeply?

48. How do you distinguish between intuition and fear?

49. What role does prayer or meditation play in your life?

50. How do you nurture your spiritual health?

51. What is the most important moral value for you, and why?

52. How do you find a balance between your spiritual beliefs and everyday actions?

53. What is a mystery that you embrace as part of your spirituality?

54. How has mindfulness made you a better person?

55. Describe an instance where a spiritual insight came to you unexpectedly.

56. What aspect of your spiritual journey are you most thankful for?

57. How do you approach learning about new spiritual concepts?

58. What does healing mean to you in a spiritual sense?

59. How do you support others in their spiritual journeys?

60. What question do you most seek an answer to in your spiritual or mindful practice?

ENVIRONMENTAL AWARENESS QUESTIONS

1. How do you define environmental awareness in your own words?

2. What was the first environmental issue that ever caught your attention?

3. How do you incorporate sustainability into your daily life?

4. What is your biggest concern about the environment today?

5. Describe a habit you've changed to be more environmentally friendly.

6. What renewable energy sources are you most interested in, and why?

7. How do you conserve water in your home or garden?

8. What are your thoughts on the use of plastics and their alternatives?

9. How do you educate yourself about environmental issues?

10. Have you ever volunteered for any environmental causes? Describe your experience.

11. What is one environmental documentary that profoundly impacted you?

12. How do you reduce your carbon footprint when traveling?

13. What sustainable products have you switched to recently?

14. Describe a local environmental issue that concerns you.

15. How do you feel about the future of the planet?

16. What steps do you take to reduce household waste?

17. How do you encourage others to be more environmentally conscious?

18. What role does politics play in your perspective on environmental issues?

19. Have you ever took part in a protest or movement toward environmental change?

20. What is the most challenging aspect of maintaining an eco-friendly lifestyle?

21. How does your workplace contribute to environmental sustainability?

22. What is your stance on wildlife conservation?

23. How do you feel about the use of pesticides and herbicides?

24. What actions do you take to support local and sustainable food sources?

25. How has your attitude towards environmental conservation developed over time?

26. What do you think is the most misunderstood environmental issue?

27. How do you balance economic growth with environmental protection?

28. What changes would you like to see in your community's approach to the environment?

29. How do you deal with eco-anxiety or feelings of overwhelm about environmental degradation?

30. What sustainable fashion choices do you make?

31. Describe an environmentally friendly project you would like to start.

32. How do you preserve nature when enjoying outdoor activities?

33. What is the most significant environmental challenge in your area?

34. How do you use technology to aid in your environmental efforts?

35. What is one simple environmental act you wish everyone would practice?

36. How do you conserve energy at home or at work?

37. Describe your dream green living space.

38. What are your views on organic farming and gardening?

39. How do you think climate change will impact future generations?

40. What are your thoughts on water conservation and management?

41. How do you think individual actions contribute to larger environmental impacts?

42. What sustainable transportation methods do you use or advocate for?

43. How do you ensure that your investments or savings are environmentally responsible?

44. What challenges do you face when trying to live sustainably?

45. How does nature inspire you?

46. What are your views on the recycling and reuse of materials?

47. Describe an instance where you had to defend your environmental beliefs.

48. How do you stay motivated to continue your environmental efforts despite setbacks?

49. What environmental policy do you wish your government would enact?

50. How do you celebrate Earth Day or other environmental holidays?

51. What is your opinion on global environmental cooperation and agreements?

52. How has your cultural background influenced your views on the environment?

53. What sustainable home improvements have you made or plan to make?

54. What is the most rewarding aspect of living an environmentally conscious life?

55. How do you approach discussions about the environment with skeptics?

56. What is your favorite nature reserve or national park, and why?

57. How do you think technology can help solve environmental issues?

58. What is one environmental myth you want to debunk?

59. How do you feel about the relationship between human health and environmental health?

60. What is one small daily action you believe can make a significant environmental difference?

ART AND CULTURE QUESTIONS

1. What piece of art has profoundly impacted your life?

2. How do you engage with the arts in your community?

3. What is your favorite art form to experience, and why?

4. Describe a cultural event that left a lasting impression on you.

5. How has your cultural background influenced your appreciation of the arts?

6. What is the last museum or gallery you visited, and what did you take away from it?

7. Who is your favorite artist, and how do they inspire you?

8. What is your earliest memory of experiencing art?

9. How do you think art influences society?

10. What role does music play in your life?

11. Describe a book that changed your perspective on an important issue.

12. What is the most culturally diverse place you have visited?

13. How has a particular culture different from your own captured your interest?

14. What piece of art do you most desire to see in person?

15. What does the term 'cultural heritage' mean to you?

16. How do you express yourself creatively?

17. What art form do you wish you were more knowledgeable about?

18. Describe a piece of literature that mirrors your life.

19. What is your favorite cultural festival or tradition?

20. How has traveling influenced your understanding of art?

21. What film has significantly altered your viewpoint?

22. What is the most thought-provoking play or performance you have ever seen?

23. How do you support local artists?

24. What is the most controversial piece of art you have encountered?

25. How does architecture impact your mood or thoughts when visiting a new place?

26. What cultural skills or craft have you learned recently?

27. How has digital media influenced your interaction with art?

28. Describe how education or experience corrected a cultural misconception you had.

29. What is the importance of preserving cultural heritage?

30. How do art and politics intersect in your view?

31. What is the most unusual art form you have come across?

32. How do you incorporate elements of your culture into daily life?

33. What is your favorite quote from a cultural figure?
34. What is your opinion on the globalization of culture?
35. How do you reconcile cultural differences in art interpretation?
36. What is your stance on the commercialization of art?
37. Describe an instance where art helped you through a difficult time.
38. What do you think the future of art looks like?
39. How do you think technology is reshaping cultural expressions?
40. What art piece do you think everyone should see, and why?
41. What song lyrics have deeply resonated with you, and in what way?
42. How has a specific cultural experience broadened your horizons?
43. What traditional art forms do you find most fascinating?
44. How do societal changes affect your perception of classic artworks?
45. What does it mean to be culturally literate in today's world?
46. How has your taste in art changed as you've aged?
47. What role does art play in education, from your perspective?
48. Describe when cultural art moved you emotionally.
49. What is the most innovative modern art form you've encountered?
50. How do you view the role of censorship in art?
51. What traditional cultural stories are important to you, and why?
52. How has your understanding of your own culture deepened through art?
53. What foreign language film or book has impacted you?
54. What artist or cultural leader would you like to have dinner with, and what would you discuss?
55. How do you think art contributes to community cohesion?
56. Describe a piece of art that you found challenging or difficult to appreciate.
57. What cultural artifact do you find most intriguing?
58. How has art influenced your personal relationships?
59. What upcoming cultural event are you most looking forward to?
60. What do you believe is the role of the artist in society?

COMMUNITY AND SOCIETY QUESTIONS

1. What does community mean to you?
2. How do you contribute to your local community?
3. What social issue is most important to you currently?
4. How has your community shaped your identity?
5. What is the biggest challenge facing your community today?
6. Describe when you felt a strong sense of belonging to a community.
7. What role do you play in your community?
8. How do you engage with issues of social justice?
9. What changes would you like to see in your local community?
10. How has your perspective on your community changed over the years?

11. What cultural traditions in your community do you cherish most?

12. How do you think individuals can best support their communities?

13. Describe a community leader who inspires you.

14. How do you handle conflicts within your community?

15. What is the most rewarding aspect of community involvement for you?

16. How do you balance personal freedom and social responsibility?

17. What community event do you look forward to annually?

18. How has a local issue affected your life personally?

19. What does being a good neighbor mean to you?

20. How do you promote inclusivity in your community?

21. How has your community responded to a crisis?

22. What historical event has significantly shaped your community?

23. How do you educate yourself about your community's needs?

24. What societal norms do you challenge?

25. How do you think your community influences your worldview?

26. Describe a time when you advocated for change in your community.

27. What local problem do you wish more people were aware of?

28. How do you foster connections with people different from you?

29. What are the benefits of living in a diverse society?

30. How do you approach discussions about sensitive societal issues?

31. What public service do you find most valuable in your community?

32. How do you think communities can better handle environmental issues?

33. What role does art play in your community?

34. How do you perceive the relationship between law enforcement and your community?

35. What measures do you take to ensure your safety in your community?

36. How has technology impacted your interactions within your community?

37. What is the biggest misconception about your community?

38. How do you deal with the generational gap in community views and values?

39. How do you think education impacts societal development?

40. Describe a cultural festival in your community and its significance.

41. What societal pressures do you feel most acutely?

42. How does your community handle the needs of its vulnerable populations?

43. How do you react to changes within your community?

44. What traditions from your community do you pass on to others?

45. How has globalization affected your local culture?

46. What do you think is the most effective way to solve disagreements in society?

47. How do you contribute to the economic welfare of your community?

48. Describe an act of kindness you witnessed in your community.

49. What role do elderly people play in your community?

50. How does your community celebrate successes?

51. What have you learned from the children in your community?

52. How do you use public spaces in your community?

53. What is your favorite local shop or business, and why?
54. How has migration affected your community?
55. What local policy would you change if you could?
56. How do you preserve your cultural heritage within a multicultural society?
57. What aspect of your community are you most proud of?
58. How do you think your community will change in the next decade?
59. How does your community support mental health?
60. What lesson have you learned from being a part of your community?

LEADERSHIP AND MANAGEMENT QUESTIONS

1. How do you define effective leadership?
2. What qualities do you think makes a good leader?
3. Can you describe a time when you had to lead a team? What was the outcome?
4. How do you handle decision-making under pressure?
5. What leadership role has taught you the most about yourself?
6. How do you motivate others?
7. What is the most challenging aspect of managing a team?
8. How do you develop trust within your team?
9. What book on leadership has significantly influenced your style?
10. How do you handle criticism and feedback as a leader?
11. What strategies do you use to manage conflict?
12. Describe a leadership failure and what you learned from it.
13. How do you balance authority and empathy in your leadership role?
14. What is your approach to delegation?
15. How do you keep your team motivated during difficult times?
16. How has your leadership style developed over your career?
17. What are your thoughts on leadership training and development?
18. How do you ensure your actions reflect your values as a leader?
19. What role does innovation play in your leadership or management style?
20. How do you handle stress and burnout as a leader?
21. Describe a mentor who has shaped your approach to leadership.
22. How do you approach mentorship within your team?
23. What methods do you use to assess your effectiveness as a leader?
24. How do you encourage creativity and innovation in your team?
25. What has been your most rewarding experience as a leader?
26. How do you navigate change management?
27. What role does emotional intelligence play in effective leadership?
28. How do you maintain your leadership development?
29. What is the biggest misconception about leadership you have encountered?
30. How do you foster a positive work environment?

31. How do you approach risk management?
32. What is the most important lesson you have learned about leadership?
33. How do you engage with other leaders in your industry or field?
34. What challenges have you faced when stepping into a leadership role?
35. How do you measure success in your leadership?
36. Describe how you've managed a high-performing individual or team.
37. What advice would you give to someone aspiring to leadership?
38. How do you ensure accountability in yourself and your team?
39. How do you deal with underperformance?
40. What impact do you hope to have as a leader?
41. How do you promote diversity and inclusion within your team?
42. How do you balance short-term and long-term goals in leadership?
43. Describe a situation where you had to be a leader outside of work.
44. What do you find most challenging about managing resources?
45. How do you prepare for a leadership role in a new project or team?
46. What traits do you admire in other leaders?
47. How do you handle the pressures of being a role model?
48. What has been your experience with leadership in a crisis?
49. How do you stay updated with new leadership theories and practices?
50. Describe how you've implemented a significant change within an organization.
51. How do you maintain work-life balance as a leader?
52. What technologies have influenced your leadership practices?
53. How do you ensure continuous improvement both personally and as a leader?
54. What role does communication play in your leadership style?
55. How do you cultivate new leaders within your organization?
56. What is the hardest decision you've had to make as a leader?
57. How do you approach ethical dilemmas in leadership?
58. What is your vision for leadership in the future of your field?
59. How do you assess the impact of your leadership on others?
60. What legacy do you hope to leave as a leader?

MUSIC AND ENTERTAINMENT QUESTIONS

1. What is your earliest memory of music?
2. Who is your all-time favorite musician or band?
3. What song always makes you feel happy?
4. Is there a movie you can watch repeatedly?
5. What was the last concert you attended?
6. How has your taste in music changed over the years?
7. What is your favorite musical genre and why?
8. What song lyrics have deeply impacted you?

9. Who is your favorite actor or actress?

10. What TV show did you last binge-watch?

11. Which book would you love to see turned into a movie or TV show?

12. What is your favorite music video?

13. How do you discover new music or movies?

14. What was the most disappointing movie you've ever seen?

15. What is your favorite song to sing in the shower?

16. Which musical instrument do you wish you could play?

17. What role does music play in your daily life?

18. What is your favorite soundtrack or score from a film?

19. Who is your favorite movie director?

20. Have you ever met a celebrity? If so, what was the experience like?

21. What is your favorite entertainment venue?

22. How do you feel about adaptations of books into movies or TV shows?

23. What is your favorite musical or play?

24. Who is your guilty pleasure artist or band?

25. What is the best live performance you've ever seen?

26. What movie or song makes you nostalgic?

27. Who would you like to see in concert that you haven't yet?

28. What is one movie or song that changed your perspective on life?

29. What is your favorite quote from a movie, song, or play?

30. What's the worst movie you've ever seen?

31. What music do you listen to when you need motivation?

32. What do you think of reality TV?

33. How does your mood affect your entertainment choices?

34. What is the funniest movie or TV show you've ever seen?

35. What book, movie, or song has made you cry?

36. Who in the entertainment industry inspires you the most, and why?

37. What is the most underrated movie, show, or band you know?

38. What is your favorite movie genre?

39. How do you prefer to watch movies: at home, on TV, streaming, or in the theater?

40. Do you have a favorite movie or TV show character? Why do you relate to them?

41. What's the last movie that surprised you?

42. How has a particular film or piece of music comforted you?

43. Do you prefer fiction or nonfiction books? Why?

44. What is your favorite comedy or drama?

45. How do you choose what to watch or listen to next?

46. What is the most influential song or movie you've experienced?

47. What piece of entertainment (book, movie, show, music) disappointed you most?

48. If you could direct a movie, what would it be about?

49. What is your favorite line from any song?

50. What film or music genre do you not like?

51. If you could write a book, what genre would it be?

52. How do entertainment choices reflect a person's personality?

53. What is your favorite dance scene from a movie or a show?

54. Which artist or band did you love as a teenager but feel differently about now?

55. What is the most powerful music concert or theater performance you've attended?

56. How do you feel about the use of music in advertising?

57. What movie or TV show world would you like to live in?

58. What's your favorite movie or music festival?

59. If you could have any director or musician's career, whose would it be?

60. What is the most interesting documentary you've watched?

HISTORICAL INFLUENCES QUESTIONS

1. What historical event has had the most profound impact on your country?

2. Which historical figure do you most admire, and why?

3. How has your family history influenced who you are today?

4. What period in history would you have liked to live in?

5. What is the most important lesson that history has taught you?

6. How do you think your life mirrors the era you grew up in?

7. What historical book has significantly influenced your view of the world?

8. Which historical event do you wish you could have witnessed?

9. How has history shaped your political beliefs?

10. What historical figure do you most identify with?

11. What ancient civilization fascinates you the most, and why?

12. How do you see the impact of past wars in today's world?

13. What family story from the past do you find most intriguing?

14. Which decade of the past century would you most like to visit, and why?

15. How has the history of art influenced your taste in aesthetics?

16. What historical film or documentary profoundly moved you?

17. How has your hometown's history influenced its culture?

18. Which historical figure's leadership style do you admire the most?

19. What lessons from history do you think are still relevant today?

20. How has migration history affected your family or community?

21. What historical event in your country do you think is most misunderstood?

22. How has history shaped your views on equality and justice?

23. What era of fashion history do you find most appealing?

24. What historical music movement do you wish you could have experienced?

25. How do you preserve your own or your family's history?

26. What historical invention do you think was the most revolutionary?

27. How has the history of science influenced current technology?

28. What history from another country do you find most interesting?

29. Which historical leader's mistakes do you think offer the biggest lessons?
30. What historical event do you think shaped the 21st century the most?
31. How do you relate personal failures and successes to historical outcomes?
32. What historical romance has captured your imagination?
33. What historical conflict do you believe had unnecessary consequences?
34. How do you think history will judge the era we live in today?
35. What is your favorite historical quote, and why does it resonate with you?
36. Which historical sport event do you find most significant?
37. How do you think past health pandemics compare to modern ones?
38. Which ancient tradition do you believe we should resurrect?
39. What is the biggest historical impact on today's educational systems?
40. How has understanding historical contexts helped you in real-life situations?
41. What historical figure do you think is overrated, and why?
42. How has the industrial revolution influenced your local community?
43. What do you think is the most significant turning point in world history?
44. How has colonial history impacted modern global relations?
45. What historical mystery do you wish someone could solve?
46. How has the evolution of language influenced modern communication?
47. What role do you think historians play in shaping the future?
48. Which historical battle do you find most fascinating?
49. How has the history of religion influenced modern spirituality?
50. What is your view on the preservation of historical monuments?
51. How has your personal history shaped your career choices?
52. What historical trend do you see reemerging in society today?
53. What is the most impactful piece of ancient philosophy on modern life?
54. How do you use historical knowledge to inform your voting decisions?
55. What role does nostalgia play in your appreciation of history?
56. How has the civil rights movement influenced your views on human rights?
57. What historical event has shaped your local community's identity?
58. How has the history of exploration influenced modern travel?
59. What historical figure would you choose to write a biography on?
60. How do you think the future generations will view our current times?

COMEDY AND HUMOR QUESTIONS

1. What makes you laugh no matter what?
2. Who is your favorite comedian and why?
3. Can you remember a time when you laughed so hard you cried?
4. What TV comedy show do you find absolutely hilarious?
5. What is the funniest movie you've ever seen?
6. How do you use humor to cope with stress?

7. What is your favorite joke to tell?

8. How does your sense of humor compare to your family's?

9. Do you have a funny memory from your childhood you can share?

10. What's the most embarrassing thing that's happened to you that you can now laugh about?

11. How do you feel about practical jokes?

12. What internet meme has made you laugh recently?

13. Who in your life always makes you laugh?

14. Do you enjoy making others laugh?

15. How important is humor in your relationships?

16. What is your favorite comedic book?

17. How has your sense of humor developed over time?

18. Do you enjoy stand-up comedy? What was the last stand-up show you saw?

19. What role does humor play in your workplace?

20. Can you share a funny miscommunication story?

21. What TV show or movie do you watch for comfort because it always makes you chuckle?

22. Have you ever been to a comedy club? Describe the experience.

23. What type of humor do you enjoy most (satire, slapstick, puns, etc.)?

24. How do you feel about dark humor?

25. What's the funniest thing you've overheard someone say?

26. Who is your favorite cartoon character or comic strip?

27. Have you ever laughed at an inappropriate time? What happened?

28. What song has funny lyrics that you love?

29. Do you have a funny habit?

30. What's the funniest gift you've ever received?

31. How do you feel about sitcoms versus sketch shows?

32. What is the silliest situation you've ever found yourself in?

33. How does humor help you in your daily life?

34. Do you like telling stories that make people laugh?

35. What's your go-to funny story to tell at parties?

36. How do you incorporate humor into your social media?

37. What funny childhood nickname did you have?

38. Do you enjoy humorous podcasts? Can you recommend one?

39. What is the funniest word in your opinion, and why?

40. How do you react to people who don't share your sense of humor?

41. What is a funny scene from a non-comedy film that you love?

42. How do you think humor connects people?

43. What's your favorite type of comedy film (rom-com, black comedy, parody, etc.)?

44. Do you think you have a good sense of timing in telling jokes?

45. How do you feel about comedians getting political in their humor?

46. What's the funniest way you've seen someone handle a mistake?

47. Have you ever tried writing your own jokes or comedic material?

48. What's a funny tradition in your family?

49. Do you think animals can be funny? Describe a humorous moment with a pet.

50. How do you feel about internet humor and memes influencing modern comedy?

51. What's a funny habit or quirk of someone you know?

52. Have you ever laughed until it hurt? What was so funny?

53. What board game do you find hilariously fun?

54. How do you feel about comedy that pushes boundaries or is controversial?

55. What's the funniest performance you've ever seen live?

56. How does humor aid in your mental health?

57. Do you think you could ever perform stand-up comedy?

58. How does humor blend with other elements in movies or shows you enjoy?

59. Do you find humor in everyday life? Give an example.

60. What humorous advice would you give to your younger self?

FOOD AND CUISINE QUESTIONS

1. What is your earliest food memory?

2. What dish reminds you of home and why?

3. What is the most unusual food you have ever tried?

4. Who in your life influenced your cooking the most?

5. What is your favorite comfort food?

6. How does your cultural background influence your cooking?

7. What is the most challenging dish you have ever prepared?

8. What is your favorite restaurant and what do you usually order there?

9. What ingredients could you not live without?

10. How has your taste in food changed as you've grown older?

11. What is your favorite international cuisine?

12. What is the best meal you've ever eaten?

13. What food do you love others might find a bit odd?

14. Have you ever taken a cooking class? What did you learn?

15. What is your go-to recipe for special occasions?

16. How do you incorporate healthy eating into your lifestyle?

17. What's the story behind your favorite recipe?

18. Have you ever had a kitchen disaster? What happened?

19. What role does food play in your social life?

20. What is your favorite food-related tradition?

21. What food have you never eaten but would really like to try?

22. What is the most memorable meal you've had while traveling?

23. How do you feel about food trends like plant-based diets?

24. What's the most important meal of the day for you?

25. Do you prefer dining out or cooking at home?

26. What's your favorite cooking show or food-related book?

27. What food do you dislike and why?
28. How has the food industry changed over the years?
29. What is your favorite type of dessert?
30. How do you decide what to cook for dinner?
31. What is your favorite seasonal dish?
32. What's the last recipe you cooked you found online?
33. Do you have any food allergies or dietary restrictions?
34. What is the role of food in your family gatherings?
35. How do you handle differences in food preferences when cooking for others?
36. What is the best cooking tip you've ever received?
37. Describe a food experience that was meaningful.
38. What's your favorite herb or spice?
39. What's the biggest risk you've taken in the kitchen?
40. How do you organize your recipes?
41. What food reminds you of your childhood?
42. Have you ever took part in a food competition?
43. What's your strategy for grocery shopping?
44. How do you experiment with new flavors and ingredients?
45. What's the most heartwarming cooking experience you've had?
46. How has your perception of food and its preparation evolved?
47. What food do you find comforting during stressful times?
48. What is your approach to portion control?
49. How do you balance taste with nutrition?
50. What food-related skill are you most proud of developing?
51. Do you have any food traditions that are unique to your family?
52. How do you make your favorite dish healthier?
53. What food did you dislike as a child but enjoy now?
54. What do you think your eating habits say about you?
55. How do you celebrate with food?
56. What's the most complex dish you've successfully cooked?
57. What is your philosophy on leftovers?
58. What kitchen gadget could you not live without?
59. How do you feel about sharing meals with others?
60. What are your thoughts on organic versus non-organic foods?

FITNESS AND SPORTS QUESTIONS

1. What is your favorite physical activity, and why do you enjoy it?
2. How does regular exercise impact your mood and mental health?
3. What sport have you always wanted to try but haven't yet?
4. Describe a memorable moment from participating in a sports event.

5. How do you motivate yourself on days when you don't feel like exercising?

6. What fitness achievement are you most proud of?

7. How do you integrate fitness into your daily routine?

8. What role do sports play in your life?

9. Have you ever experienced a sports injury? How did you recover and what did you learn?

10. What is your preferred type of workout: cardio, strength, flexibility, or a combination?

11. How has your approach to fitness changed over the years?

12. What is the most challenging physical activity you have ever done?

13. Who is your sports hero, and what qualities do you admire in them?

14. What is one fitness goal you are currently working towards?

15. How do you balance fitness with other responsibilities in your life?

16. What is your favorite piece of workout equipment or apparel?

17. How do team sports differ from individual sports in your experience?

18. What sport or fitness activity have you recently discovered and loved?

19. How does the weather affect your exercise routine?

20. What is the best fitness advice you have ever received?

21. How do you deal with setbacks like plateaus or loss of motivation in fitness?

22. Describe how taking part in sports has shaped your teamwork skills.

23. What is your favorite sports-related memory?

24. How do you use technology to enhance your fitness experience?

25. What are your thoughts on competitive versus recreational sports?

26. How do you ensure proper nutrition for your fitness needs?

27. What misconceptions about fitness have you encountered?

28. How has fitness or sports taught you about discipline and perseverance?

29. What fitness trend do you find intriguing right now?

30. How does your community or culture view fitness and sports?

31. How do you celebrate achievements in your fitness journey?

32. What is the biggest challenge you face in maintaining an active lifestyle?

33. How do you incorporate recovery and rest into your fitness regimen?

34. What advice would you give someone starting their fitness journey?

35. How does fitness contribute to your sense of self-esteem?

36. What is your favorite sport to watch, and do you prefer to watch it live or on TV?

37. How do you stay active during travel or vacation?

38. What impact has your fitness journey had on your social life?

39. How do you handle the financial costs associated with sports or fitness activities?

40. What fitness or sports activity do you find the most relaxing?

41. How do you handle differences in fitness or sports interests with your partner or family?

42. What is the role of a coach or trainer in your sports life?

43. How do you prepare mentally and physically for a sports competition?

44. What sport do you think everyone should try at least once?

45. How has your fitness routine helped you cope with stress?

46. What are your favorite sports documentaries or movies?

47. How do you deal with fear or anxiety when trying a new sport or fitness challenge?
48. What are the benefits of outdoor versus indoor exercise for you?
49. How do you manage dietary needs in relation to fitness?
50. In your opinion, which sport or fitness activity is underrated?
51. How has being an athlete or physically active person influenced your professional life?
52. What are your thoughts on children's participation in competitive sports?
53. How do cultural attitudes towards fitness impact your approach?
54. What is one sport or fitness fad you think is overrated?
55. How do you recover from a disappointing performance or result in a sports event?
56. What role does the community play in your fitness or sports activities?
57. How do you track progress in your fitness or sports skills?
58. What changes have you made to your fitness routine as you've aged?
59. How does fitness influence your plans for the future?
60. What lessons have you learned from sports that apply to other areas of your life?

PERSONAL CHALLENGES QUESTIONS

1. What is the most significant challenge you have overcome in your life?
2. How did you manage stress during a difficult time?
3. Can you describe a time when you failed at something important to you?
4. What did you learn about yourself from your last major challenge?
5. How do you motivate yourself to keep going when things get tough?
6. What personal limitations have you discovered through your challenges?
7. How has a challenge changed your perspective on life?
8. What strategies do you find most effective for handling pressure?
9. Who do you turn to for support during difficult times?
10. How do you prioritize self-care when facing personal challenges?
11. What challenge are you currently facing, and how are you dealing with it?
12. Have you ever had to make a tough decision under stress? How did you decide?
13. What personal strengths have you developed through overcoming challenges?
14. How do you prepare mentally for a challenge?
15. What role does resilience play in your life?
16. Can you share an experience where you turned a failure into a learning opportunity?
17. How do you handle uncertainty and unpredictability in challenging situations?
18. What challenge have you avoided, and why?
19. How do you measure personal success when facing challenges?
20. What advice would you give someone going through a similar challenge as yours?
21. How has overcoming a personal challenge affected your relationships?
22. What fears have you conquered in recent years?
23. In what ways have you had to adapt to overcome a challenge?
24. How do you maintain balance during life's ups and downs?

25. What has been your toughest emotional challenge?

26. How do you rebuild confidence after someone shakes it?

27. What personal challenge has brought unexpected benefits?

28. How do you celebrate overcoming a challenge?

29. What book or resource has helped you manage tough times?

30. How do you stay grounded when facing personal adversity?

31. What challenge has taught you the most about compassion and empathy?

32. How do you keep your spirit up during long-term challenges?

33. What practices help you maintain clarity and focus in tough situations?

34. How has your approach to challenges changed as you've aged?

35. What is the most challenging aspect of your personal or professional life right now?

36. How do you deal with setbacks?

37. What personal habits help you deal with challenges effectively?

38. What is the biggest risk you've taken to overcome a challenge?

39. How do you assess and manage risks when facing tough decisions?

40. How do you handle the stress of not meeting your own expectations?

41. What has been the hardest part of growing older for you?

42. How do you recognize when to push through a challenge versus when to walk away?

43. What lesson took you the longest to learn regarding personal challenges?

44. How do you use your experiences to help others with their challenges?

45. What challenge have you overcome that you once thought impossible?

46. How do you maintain hope during difficult phases of life?

47. How have your challenges shaped your view on mental health?

48. What misconceptions about handling challenges do you think most people have?

49. How do you differentiate between a challenge that grows you and one that harms you?

50. What role does gratitude play in overcoming challenges?

51. How do you apply past lessons to new challenges?

52. What's the most unconventional method you've used to overcome an obstacle?

53. How do you handle the fear of the unknown?

54. What part of your personal identity has been most shaped by challenges?

55. How do you prepare for potential challenges when planning for the future?

56. What is the most physically demanding challenge you've faced?

57. How do challenges in your personal life affect your professional life, and vice versa?

58. What challenge are you proud of but rarely speak about?

59. How do you decompress after a particularly stressful period?

60. Looking back, which challenge are you most grateful for?

PETS AND ANIMALS QUESTIONS

1. What was your first pet, and what special memories do you have of them?

2. How do pets improve your daily life?

3. Do you prefer domesticated pets or wild animals? Why?

4. Describe an encounter with a wild animal that left a lasting impression on you.

5. How do you feel about zoos and aquariums?

6. Have you ever volunteered at an animal shelter? What was that experience like?

7. What responsibilities come with owning a pet that people often overlook?

8. What animal best represents your personality and why?

9. How do you feel about the ethics of pet breeding?

10. What measures do you take to ensure your pets are happy and healthy?

11. Have you ever had to deal with the loss of a pet? How did you cope?

12. What's the most unusual pet you have ever met or heard about?

13. How do you think society can improve animal welfare?

14. Do you believe pets have emotions like humans? Why or why not?

15. How do you balance the needs of pets with the needs of human family members?

16. What's your stance on keeping exotic animals as pets?

17. How has having pets affected your family or household dynamics?

18. What's the funniest thing a pet has ever done in your presence?

19. How do pets contribute to your mental and emotional well-being?

20. What's one animal-related activity or hobby you enjoy (e.g., bird watching, horse riding)?

21. Do you have a preferred veterinarian or pet care professional? What makes them trustworthy?

22. How do you educate yourself about the proper care of pets?

23. What's the most challenging aspect of pet ownership?

24. What wildlife conservation issues are you most passionate about?

25. How do animals inspire creativity in your life?

26. What are your views on using animals in entertainment (circuses, races, etc.)?

27. Describe a lesson you've learned from observing or interacting with animals.

28. How do you feel about the use of animals in scientific research?

29. Have pets or animals influenced your career choices or hobbies in any way?

30. What role do animals play in your favorite books or movies?

31. How do you react to people who don't treat animals well?

32. What's your approach to training and disciplining pets?

33. How do you include pets in family celebrations or holidays?

34. What are your thoughts on pet insurance?

35. Have you ever helped an injured or lost animal? What happened?

36. What's your favorite animal charity or cause, and why?

37. How do pets help you connect with other people?

38. What has owning a pet taught you about responsibility?

39. What's the most rewarding part of caring for a pet?

40. How do you feel about pets sleeping in bed with their owners?

41. What's your favorite outdoor activity to do with your pet?

42. How do you handle disagreements about pet care with family or roommates?

43. Have you ever had a pet with special needs? What was that experience like?

44. What's the biggest sacrifice you've made for your pet?

45. How do you ensure your pets get enough physical activity?
46. What's your favorite animal-themed piece of clothing or accessory?
47. How do pets affect your daily routine?
48. What considerations would you advise someone to think about before getting a pet?
49. How do you feel about using technology to track or monitor pets?
50. What's the most important thing a pet has taught you?
51. Have you ever been involved in a pet rescue operation?
52. What's the most memorable journey you've taken with a pet?
53. How do pets and animals feature in your favorite artistic works (paintings, sculptures, etc.)?
54. What's your stance on pet diets and feeding natural foods versus commercial pet food?
55. How do you deal with allergies or phobias related to animals in your home?
56. What's your view on licensing and regulations for pet ownership?
57. Have pets influenced your perspectives on nature and the environment?
58. How do you prepare to care for pets during emergencies or disasters?
59. What cultural significance do animals hold for you or your community?
60. How do you think future generations will treat and interact with pets and wildlife?

SCIENCE AND INNOVATION QUESTIONS

1. What scientific discovery has significantly impacted your life?
2. How do you stay updated with the latest technological advancements?
3. What piece of modern technology can you not imagine living without?
4. How do you think artificial intelligence will affect your future?
5. What ethical considerations do you think are important in genetic engineering?
6. What is your opinion on the role of technology in education?
7. How has the internet changed the way you learn and access information?
8. What innovation do you think will most dramatically shape the next decade?
9. How do you balance privacy and convenience when using new technology?
10. What are your thoughts on the use of drones in society?
11. How has mobile technology changed your daily interactions?
12. What science fiction technology do you wish existed today?
13. What role does sustainability play in your views on innovation?
14. What scientific field are you most curious about and why?
15. How do you think space exploration impacts humanity's future?
16. What are your thoughts on the development of renewable energy technologies?
17. How has social media influenced your understanding of the world?
18. What technological advancement has improved your health or fitness?
19. How do you feel about the merging of human biology with technology?
20. What do you believe is the most pressing scientific issue facing society?
21. How has technology affected your career or industry?
22. What do you think about the pace of technological change?

23. How do you use technology to enhance your creativity?
24. What challenges do you think science will solve in your lifetime?
25. How do you approach skepticism towards science and technology?
26. What role should governments play in regulating new technologies?
27. How do you think virtual reality will grow in the coming years?
28. What innovation has changed the way you manage your personal finances?
29. How has technology affected your relationships with others?
30. What do you think about the long-term impacts of kids growing up with technology?
31. What recent scientific research or study has caught your interest?
32. How do you discern reliable scientific information from misinformation?
33. What technological device do you think needs radical improvement?
34. How do you feel about the security of your online data?
35. What impacts do you think telemedicine will have on healthcare?
36. How do you feel about the use of technology in policing and security?
37. What advancements in transportation technology excite you the most?
38. How do you think climate change science will evolve?
39. What are your views on integrating artificial intelligence in everyday life?
40. How has wearable technology influenced your lifestyle?
41. What is the most fascinating element of quantum computing to you?
42. How do you perceive the future of robotics in the workplace?
43. What are your thoughts on tech companies' influence in global politics?
44. How do you ensure you adapt to new technologies?
45. What do you think are the societal implications of biotechnology?
46. How do you view the relationship between technology and art?
47. What steps do you take to reduce your digital footprint?
48. What do you think about the use of technology in sports?
49. How do you feel about the potential for 3D printing in your life?
50. What are the ethical considerations of surveillance technology in public spaces?
51. How do you think augmented reality will impact professional training?
52. What are your thoughts on technology's role in personal wellness?
53. How do you think technology will change the way we eat?
54. What scientific experiment would you conduct if resources were not an issue?
55. How do you think advancements in science will impact religion or spirituality?
56. What role does citizen science play in today's society?
57. How do you think technologies in entertainment will evolve?
58. What do you think about the intersection of technology and privacy?
59. How do you feel about the pace of change in medical technology?
60. What do you foresee as the next big trend in technology and innovation?

FANTASY AND IMAGINATION QUESTIONS

1. What fictional world would you choose to live in if you had the chance?
2. Who is your favorite fictional character, and why do you resonate with them?
3. If you could possess any magical power, what would it be and why?
4. Describe a recurring dream you have. What do you think it means?
5. How has your imagination influenced your career or personal life?
6. What is the most imaginative book you've ever read?
7. If you could invent anything, what would it be and how would it impact the world?
8. Describe an imaginary friend you had as a child or a character you created.
9. What does your ideal fantasy vacation look like and why?
10. If you could meet any author of a fantasy novel, who would it be and what would you ask them?
11. What mythological creature do you wish existed?
12. How do you use your imagination to solve problems?
13. Describe a fantasy you often indulge in when daydreaming.
14. What fairy tale did you love most growing up, and how has it influenced you?
15. If you could design a world, what three rules would govern it?
16. What kind of superhero would you be and what would be your backstory?
17. Describe the plot of a movie you wish someone would make.
18. How do you think advancing technology could bring us closer to living in a fantasy world?
19. What role does imagination play in your relationships?
20. How would you use a time machine, both in fictional and practical terms?
21. What's the most imaginative artwork you've ever seen?
22. If you could live in any era of history as a different person, who would you choose to be?
23. Describe your perfect imaginary pet.
24. What imaginary sport would you like to compete in?
25. How has a film or artwork transported you to another place mentally?
26. If you were a wizard, what would be your signature spell?
27. How do you incorporate elements of fantasy into your everyday life?
28. What enchanted item from a book or movie do you wish you owned?
29. Who is your favorite villain from a book or movie, and what makes them interesting?
30. How does fantasy or science fiction influence your worldview?
31. What futuristic invention do you hope becomes a reality in your lifetime?
32. If you could switch lives with a character in any TV show or movie for a day, who would it be and why?
33. What's the strangest dream you've ever had?
34. How do you creatively express yourself?
35. What fictional job would you want to have?
36. Describe a place that you've visited that felt like it was out of a fantasy world.
37. What's the most imaginative gift you've ever received?
38. If you could create a new holiday, what would it celebrate and how?

39. What's the most creative story you've ever come up with?

40. How would you survive a zombie apocalypse based on the books/movies you know?

41. What character from a children's book do you still think about?

42. If you could have dinner with any fictional character, who would it be and what would you talk about?

43. How has a piece of music transported you to a different realm?

44. If magic was real, how do you think our world would be different?

45. What's the most surprising plot twist you've encountered in a story?

46. How do you think the ability to dream affects our lives?

47. What would your fantasy alter ego be like?

48. Describe the best costume you've ever worn.

49. If you could design a virtual reality world, what would it include?

50. What fictional family would you want to be part of?

51. If you could transform into any animal, which one would you choose and why?

52. What legendary or historical figure do you most identify with?

53. What's the most elaborate fantasy or game you've ever played?

54. How would you use a magical wand in your daily life?

55. If you could speak or understand any language, real or fictional, which would you choose?

56. Describe the fantasy character you created for a game or story.

57. What enchanted object from a book or movie do you wish you could use just once?

58. If you were to write a book, what fantasy elements would you include?

59. How do you think growing up with fantasy stories influences a person's creativity?

60. What is the greatest adventure you can imagine going on?

FASHION AND STYLE QUESTIONS

1. How would you describe your personal style in three words?

2. What is your favorite piece of clothing, and why is it special?

3. Who is your fashion icon, and what do you admire about their style?

4. How has your style developed over the past decade?

5. What is the most daring fashion trend you have ever tried?

6. What item in your wardrobe do you wear the most, and why?

7. How do you decide what to wear for a big event?

8. What was your biggest fashion regret?

9. How does your style reflect your personality?

10. What fashion rule do you think is outdated?

11. What is the most expensive piece of clothing you've ever purchased, and was it worth it?

12. How do you feel about second-hand and vintage clothing?

13. What does sustainable fashion mean to you, and how do you incorporate it into your life?

14. What is one clothing item you would never wear?

15. How do you organize your wardrobe?

16. What is your approach to choosing outfits each day?
17. How has your cultural background influenced your fashion choices?
18. What is the oldest item in your wardrobe, and why have you kept it?
19. How do you balance comfort with style?
20. What fashion trend do you love right now?
21. How important are brand names to you when shopping for clothes?
22. What piece of fashion advice would you give to your younger self?
23. How does the season influence your style choices?
24. What is your favorite accessory, and what does it say about you?
25. How do you handle trends you like but don't feel suit you?
26. What is your favorite fashion era, and would you ever dress like that today?
27. How do you decide which new trends to follow?
28. What impact do you think fashion has on society?
29. How do you define the difference between fashion and style?
30. What fashion-related book or movie do you find most inspirational?
31. How do you mix and match colors and patterns in your outfits?
32. What is the most comfortable outfit you own?
33. How do you use clothing to change or enhance your mood?
34. What style do you appreciate on others but never wear yourself?
35. How do you incorporate unique or unconventional items into your outfits?
36. What role does jewelry play in your personal style?
37. How do you feel about custom-made clothing?
38. Do you prefer to shop online or in stores, and why?
39. What piece of clothing makes you feel most confident?
40. How do you feel about wearing uniforms or having a dress code?
41. What is the biggest challenge you face when shopping for clothes?
42. How do you decide when it's time to retire a piece of clothing?
43. What style advice would you give someone looking to redefine their look?
44. How do you keep your style fresh without constantly buying new clothes?
45. What's the most unique piece of clothing you own, and what's the story behind it?
46. How does your work attire differ from your casual or weekend attire?
47. What role do shoes play in your overall look?
48. How do you care for and maintain your clothes?
49. What fashion mistake is a deal-breaker for you?
50. How do you deal with the pressure of looking a certain way in social or professional settings?
51. What's your strategy for dressing on a tight budget?
52. How does fashion influence your perception of others?
53. How do you express creativity through your clothing?
54. What's a recent fashion discovery (brand, style, trend) you're excited about?
55. How do you handle the change of seasons in your wardrobe?
56. What is one fashion item you splurge on?
57. How do you incorporate fitness and comfort into your style?

58. What fashion blogs, magazines, or influencers do you follow for inspiration?
59. How has your style impacted your relationships or social interactions?
60. What does fashion mean to you beyond just clothing?

GAMES AND RECREATION QUESTIONS

1. What is your earliest memory of playing games?
2. What board game do you always enjoy, and why?
3. What video game has had the most significant impact on you?
4. What recreational activity do you find most relaxing?
5. How competitive are you when it comes to sports or games?
6. What is your favorite outdoor activity?
7. What is your most memorable experience at a sporting event?
8. What card game do you excel at, and who taught you to play?
9. How has your taste in games and recreation changed over the years?
10. What is your favorite family game night memory?
11. What sport do you enjoy watching the most, and why?
12. What game do you think teaches an important life lesson?
13. What recreational hobby have you recently picked up?
14. What is your favorite mobile game and what do you enjoy about it?
15. What role do games play in your social life?
16. How do you balance screen time with physical recreation?
17. What traditional game from your culture do you cherish?
18. What's the most challenging game you've ever played?
19. Describe a time when playing a game taught you something surprising about someone else.
20. What recreational skills are you currently trying to improve?
21. What is your go-to activity for de-stressing after a long week?
22. Have you ever invented a game? Describe it.
23. What is your favorite workout or physical fitness game?
24. What game do you wish you could master?
25. What is the funniest game you've ever played?
26. How do you feel about puzzle games or brain teasers?
27. What water sport or activity do you enjoy the most?
28. What is your favorite way to spend time outdoors?
29. What game or sport has strengthened bonds with your friends or family?
30. What is the most adventurous recreational activity you've tried?
31. How do you incorporate play into your daily routine?
32. What recreational clubs or groups are you a part of?
33. What game or sport do you wish was more popular?
34. What role does strategy play in your favorite games?
35. How do you prefer to celebrate wins in competitive situations?

36. What's a game that you enjoy that is relatively unknown?

37. Do you have a collection related to any games or recreational hobbies?

38. How do you feel about team sports versus individual sports?

39. What's the longest you've ever spent playing a game in one sitting?

40. What game from your childhood would you bring back for today's kids?

41. Have games or sports ever helped you overcome a difficult time in your life?

42. What is the most physically demanding game or sport you've taken part in?

43. How do you feel about the luck vs. skill debate in gaming?

44. What recreational activity do you wish you could do more often?

45. What is the most unusual recreational activity you've heard of or tried?

46. How do you approach learning a new game or sport?

47. What is your favorite spectator sport?

48. Describe a unique recreational pastime of your community or country.

49. What role do games play in your holiday traditions?

50. How do games enhance your creativity or thinking?

51. What's your favorite thing to do during a beach vacation?

52. How do you motivate yourself to stay active in recreational pursuits?

53. What is the most intricate game or sport you've learned?

54. How do you deal with losing in a competitive activity?

55. What fitness or sport-related goal are you working towards?

56. What game or recreational activity makes you feel nostalgic?

57. How has participating in sports or games improved your health?

58. What new game or sport would you like to see invented?

59. How do you incorporate games into social gatherings?

60. What is the biggest life lesson you've learned from playing games?

HEALTH AND SAFETY QUESTIONS

1. How do you prioritize your mental and physical health daily?

2. What is one health-related goal you are currently working towards?

3. How has your understanding of personal safety changed over the years?

4. What safety precautions do you take others might overlook?

5. Describe a time when a safety measure significantly impacted your life.

6. What is your strategy for maintaining a healthy work-life balance?

7. How do you stay informed about health recommendations and safety guidelines?

8. What is the most challenging aspect of managing your health?

9. How do you approach mental health in your daily routine?

10. What health advice do you wish you had followed earlier in life?

11. Describe your relationship with exercise and physical fitness.

12. How do you ensure safety in your home environment?

13. What wellness habit has made the biggest difference in your life?

14. How has your diet evolved to better support your health?
15. What misconceptions about health and safety have you encountered?
16. How do you manage stress and its impact on your health?
17. What steps do you take to cultivate a safe and supportive community?
18. How do you approach conversations about health with loved ones?
19. What safety skills do you think everyone should know?
20. How do you balance traditional and modern medicine in your healthcare?
21. What is the most important health lesson you've learned from a family member?
22. How has technology impacted your health and safety practices?
23. What changes in your health have you noticed with aging?
24. How do you prepare for health emergencies?
25. What preventative health measures do you find most effective?
26. How do you address safety concerns when traveling?
27. What role does insurance play in your health and safety planning?
28. What is your approach to holistic health practices?
29. How do you stay motivated to follow health and safety protocols?
30. What's the biggest health scare you've overcome?
31. How do you incorporate safety into your recreational activities?
32. What's your approach to vaccinations and preventive medicine?
33. How do you use digital tools to enhance your health?
34. What is your biggest concern about healthcare today?
35. How do you navigate health information and decide what to trust?
36. How do you handle the health and safety aspects of raising children?
37. What is one change you've made to your lifestyle for better health?
38. How do you ensure your physical safety in public spaces?
39. What natural remedies are part of your health regime?
40. How do you assess new health trends and fads?
41. What habits do you have in place to ensure a good night's sleep?
42. How do you educate yourself on mental health issues?
43. What safety features are essential in your vehicle?
44. How has a personal injury affected your views on safety?
45. What measures do you take to protect your skin and body from environmental hazards?
46. How do you approach dental and oral health?
47. What is your stance on the use of technology for health monitoring?
48. How do you ensure dietary balance to support your health?
49. What steps do you take to avoid burnout?
50. How do you prepare yourself and your home for natural disasters?
51. How has your approach to personal safety changed after becoming a parent?
52. What is the most valuable health-related investment you've made?
53. How do you manage health risks related to your profession?
54. What community health resources do you rely on?
55. How do you maintain safety during extreme weather?

56. What safety protocols do you find excessive or unnecessary?

57. How do you decide when to seek medical advice?

58. What is your philosophy on aging and health?

59. How do you advocate for your health needs in a medical setting?

60. What legacy of health and safety do you want to pass on to future generations?

PARENTING AND FAMILY LIFE QUESTIONS

1. What values did your parents instill in you that you've carried into your own parenting?

2. How do you balance personal aspirations with family responsibilities?

3. What is one tradition from your childhood that you've continued with your own family?

4. How has your relationship with your parents changed since you became an adult?

5. What is the most important lesson you hope to pass on to your children?

6. Describe a memorable family vacation. What made it special?

7. How do you handle disagreements in parenting styles with your partner or co-parent?

8. What aspect of your family life would you most like to improve?

9. How has becoming a parent changed your perspective on work and career?

10. What activities do you enjoy most as a family?

11. How do you make sure you spend quality time with each family member?

12. What do you find most challenging about parenting today?

13. In what ways are you like or different from your parents in terms of parenting?

14. How do you handle the stress that comes with parenting responsibilities?

15. What is your most cherished memory of family togetherness?

16. How do you teach your children about handling conflict?

17. What role does your extended family play in your everyday life?

18. How do you incorporate your cultural heritage into your family life?

19. What parenting advice did you receive that you found particularly useful or not useful?

20. How do you deal with the challenges of modern technology in your children's lives?

21. What book or resource has significantly influenced your parenting?

22. How do you approach conversations about difficult topics with your children?

23. What have you learned about yourself through parenting?

24. How do you manage work-life balance to accommodate your family's needs?

25. What hopes and fears do you have for your children's futures?

26. How do you nurture your relationship with your spouse or partner while parenting?

27. What does a typical weekend look like for your family?

28. How have you handled a major family crisis or challenge?

29. How do you ensure each child feels valued and understood?

30. What changes have you made to your lifestyle since becoming a parent?

31. How do you encourage your children to pursue their interests and passions?

32. How do you handle your emotions in front of your children when under stress?

33. What legacy do you hope to leave for your children?

34. How do you make holidays and special occasions memorable for your family?
35. What is the role of discipline in your parenting, and how do you implement it?
36. How do you foster a sense of responsibility in your children?
37. What is your approach to monitoring your children's academic progress?
38. How do you support your children through disappointments or failures?
39. What family rituals are most important to you, and why?
40. How do you handle differences in opinion within your family?
41. What is the best parenting or family life tip you've ever received?
42. How do you maintain your personal identity while fulfilling your parenting roles?
43. How do you manage sibling rivalry in your household?
44. What is one thing you wish you had known before becoming a parent?
45. How do you stay connected with your children as they grow older?
46. What are your family's rules about screen time and digital devices?
47. How do you encourage healthy eating habits in your family?
48. What steps do you take to ensure your family's safety at home and outside?
49. How has your parenting been influenced by the community or society you live in?
50. What is the funniest thing one of your children has ever said or done?
51. How do you approach teaching your children about financial responsibility?
52. How do you and your family give back to the community?
53. What are your strategies for managing busy family schedules?
54. How has your approach to parenting changed with each child?
55. How do you keep your family motivated to stay active and healthy?
56. What has been your proudest moment as a parent?
57. How do you encourage your children to form their own opinions?
58. How do you handle it when you and your partner disagree on a parenting issue?
59. What has been the most surprising aspect of family life for you?
60. How do you ensure that love and affection are openly expressed in your family?

FUTURE AND TECHNOLOGY QUESTIONS

1. How do you think technology will change the way we work in the next 10 years?
2. What emerging technology are you most excited about?
3. Do you have any concerns about the rise of artificial intelligence? What are they?
4. How has technology in your lifetime improved your daily life the most?
5. What piece of technology do you wish people had never invented?
6. How do you think virtual reality will affect everyday life in the future?
7. What is one futuristic gadget you wish existed right now?
8. How do you stay updated with technological advancements?
9. Do you think technology has made your personal relationships better or worse? Why?
10. How has the internet changed your perspective on the world?
11. What role do you think technology should play in education?

12. How do you balance the convenience of technology with privacy concerns?

13. What do you think will be the biggest challenge in managing technology's growth?

14. How do you feel about the use of drones in civilian life?

15. What science fiction movie or book do you think most accurately predicts the future?

16. How has social media influenced your views on privacy?

17. What are your thoughts on the development of self-driving cars?

18. How do you think technology impacts mental health?

19. What tech innovation has significantly impacted your industry or profession?

20. Do you think there will be a backlash against technological advancements?

21. What technology do you use every day that you could not live without?

22. How do you think technology will change the healthcare industry?

23. What do you think about the ethical implications of biotechnology?

24. How do you think technology will affect human communication in the future?

25. What steps do you take to secure your personal data online?

26. How do you think technology will impact human creativity?

27. What technology do you think will revolutionize the entertainment industry?

28. How would you like to see technology address environmental issues?

29. What are your thoughts on the pace of technological change? Is it too fast, too slow, or just right?

30. How do you foresee the role of humans changing as robots and AI become more advanced?

31. What personal task would you automate if you could?

32. What do you think about the longevity and transhumanism movements?

33. How has technology changed your consumption of news and media?

34. What do you think is the most important ethical question technology raises?

35. How would you feel about having a robot for a co-worker?

36. What kind of technology do you think will be obsolete in the next 20 years?

37. How do you feel about the possibility of colonizing other planets?

38. What are your biggest hopes for the future of technology?

39. What are your biggest fears regarding the future of technology?

40. How do you see the integration of technology and art evolving?

41. What technology do you avoid using because you feel it's unnecessary?

42. How do you think digital currencies will change the economy?

43. What technology do you think is currently underdeveloped and has more potential?

44. How has mobile technology changed your life the most?

45. Do you think technology helps or hinders your productivity? How so?

46. What do you think about the use of technology in surveillance by governments or corporations?

47. How do you feel about the potential cloning of humans?

48. What technology would you develop to improve education?

49. How has technology affected your physical health?

50. What are your thoughts on the digital divide and access to technology?

51. How has e-commerce changed your shopping habits?

52. What impact do you think automation will have on job security?

53. How comfortable are you with the idea of implantable technology?

54. What do you think about the ethical use of technology in sports?

55. How do you think augmented reality will change everyday life?

56. What tech skills do you think everyone should learn?

57. How has technology changed the way you travel?

58. What role should governments have in regulating emerging technologies?

59. How do you think technology can improve government transparency?

60. What futuristic technology do you hope your children or future generations will see become reality?

BOOKS AND LITERATURE QUESTIONS

1. What book has had the most significant impact on your life, and why?

2. Who is your favorite author, and what draws you to their work?

3. What genre do you find yourself drawn to the most?

4. Describe a book that changed your perspective on an important issue.

5. What is the most challenging book you have ever read, and what made it challenging?

6. What book do you wish everyone would read and why?

7. How do you choose the books you read?

8. What book has made you laugh out loud?

9. Have you ever read a book that made you cry? What was it?

10. What's the most interesting thing you've learned from a book recently?

11. Who in your life introduced you to reading, and how do they influence your choices now?

12. What book are you currently reading, and what motivated you to pick it up?

13. What is your all-time favorite children's book?

14. What book do you reread regularly, and what keeps bringing you back?

15. What's your favorite book-to-film adaptation?

16. Do you prefer ebooks, audiobooks, or traditional paper books? Why?

17. What book has inspired you to travel or explore a new place?

18. Who is your least favorite author, and why do their works not resonate with you?

19. What is the most underrated book you've ever read?

20. What literary character do you most identify with and why?

21. What's your favorite quote from any book?

22. What book has been on your "to read" list the longest, and why haven't you read it yet?

23. What book did you expect to dislike but ended up loving?

24. How has your taste in books changed over the years?

25. What book has significantly influenced your career or personal development?

26. What is the most memorable opening line from a book you've read?

27. What book do you think is overrated, and why?

28. Describe a book that scared you.

29. How do you share your love of books with others?

30. What is the best book you've read based on a recommendation?

31. What book have you lent out the most?

32. What do you enjoy most about your favorite literary genre?

33. What themes or topics are you drawn to in literature?

34. How do you organize your bookshelves?

35. What author, living or dead, would you like to have dinner with, and what would you discuss?

36. What book sparked your love for reading?

37. How has a particular book broadened your understanding of another culture?

38. What's the biggest book you've ever read, and what motivated you to finish it?

39. How do you decide when to abandon a book you aren't enjoying?

40. What's your favorite setting in which to read?

41. How do you balance reading time with other responsibilities?

42. What book made you think deeply about its content?

43. What is the most beautiful book you own?

44. What is your favorite classic novel and what makes it timeless?

45. Do you have a favorite literary journal or blog?

46. How do you approach reading a dense or academic book?

47. What book has helped you through a tough time?

48. What's your favorite under-the-radar author or book series?

49. How do you feel about annotated books or writing in the margins?

50. What fictional world would you most like to live in?

51. What are your reading goals for this year?

52. How do book clubs or reading groups influence your reading choices?

53. What's the funniest book you've ever read?

54. What biographies or autobiographies have you found most compelling?

55. How has your family background influenced your reading choices?

56. What book have you given as a gift most frequently?

57. What is your policy on lending books to friends or family?

58. How does reading shape your identity?

59. What upcoming book release are you most excited about?

60. How do you keep track of your reading list or books you have read?

LANGUAGE AND COMMUNICATION QUESTIONS

1. What language do you wish you could speak fluently, and why?

2. How has your communication style changed over the years?

3. What word do you find most intriguing in your native language?

4. Have you ever experienced a miscommunication that led to an important lesson?

5. What book or article significantly improved your understanding of communication?

6. How do you express affection and care in words?

7. What is the hardest part about learning a new language for you?

8. Describe a time when language barriers presented a challenge.

9. How do you adapt your communication style in a professional setting?

10. What is your approach to resolving misunderstandings in conversations?

11. Do you prefer written or spoken communication? Why?

12. What non-verbal cues are you most sensitive to?

13. How has the internet changed the way you communicate?

14. What is the most powerful speech or presentation you have ever heard?

15. How do you handle communication under stress?

16. What role does active listening play in your relationships?

17. How do you ensure clarity in your messages?

18. What is your favorite quote, and what does it communicate to you?

19. How does your cultural background influence your communication style?

20. What language or communication skill are you currently trying to improve?

21. How has a misinterpretation ever led to a positive outcome?

22. In what ways do you use language to persuade or influence others?

23. What is the most meaningful conversation you've ever had?

24. How do you feel about public speaking, and what experiences have shaped this?

25. What slang or colloquialisms from your area do you find most endearing?

26. How do you communicate differently online vs. in person?

27. What poem or song lyric has deeply affected the way you think about language?

28. What is the greatest communication challenge you've faced in a relationship?

29. How do you approach communication with someone who has opposing views?

30. How has learning a foreign language changed your perspective on the world?

31. What is the most difficult letter or email you've ever had to write?

32. How do you ensure you understand someone correctly when communicating?

33. What is one language or dialect you find beautiful? Why?

34. How do you feel about the evolution of language, such as the creation of new words?

35. What is a word you overuse, and why do you think that is?

36. How do you handle sarcasm in conversations?

37. What communication habit of others frustrates you the most?

38. How does your voice or tone change depending on the context?

39. What has been your experience with language learning apps or courses?

40. How do you express disagreement constructively?

41. What are common communication errors that you notice in others?

42. How do you think communication styles differ across generations?

43. What book or movie dialogue has stuck with you, and why?

44. How do you approach learning technical or specialized vocabulary?

45. What role does humor play in your everyday conversations?

46. How do you feel about the use of emoticons and emojis in communication?

47. What is the most important aspect of communication in maintaining friendships?

48. How do you recover from a communication blunder?

49. In what situation did you feel your communication was most effective?

50. What languages have you studied, and how have they shaped your thinking?
51. How do you approach communicating with someone from a different cultural background?
52. What are your tips for someone trying to improve their communication skills?
53. How do language skills influence your professional opportunities?
54. What is the best compliment you have received about your communication skills?
55. How do you think communication differs between intimate relationships and friendships?
56. What is the biggest barrier to effective communication you have encountered?
57. How do you encourage others to express themselves more clearly?
58. What aspect of your communication would you most like to change?
59. How do you deal with nerves when speaking in front of an audience?
60. What has been the impact of multilingualism on your personal or professional life?

TRAVEL AND EXPLORATION QUESTIONS

1. What is the most unforgettable trip you have ever taken?
2. Which destination has had the most significant impact on you, and why?
3. What is the most adventurous thing you've done while traveling?
4. How do you prepare for a trip to a place you've never visited before?
5. What's at the top of your travel bucket list, and why?
6. Describe a moment from your travels that took your breath away.
7. How has travel changed your perspective on the world?
8. What cultural practice from another country have you adopted into your own life?
9. What's the most challenging travel experience you've had, and what did it teach you?
10. Do you prefer solo travel, traveling with friends, or family vacations? Why?
11. What's your favorite travel memory with a loved one?
12. How do you balance tourist attractions with off-the-beaten-path experiences?
13. What place have you visited that felt like stepping back in time?
14. How do you deal with language barriers and cultural differences when traveling?
15. What is the best meal you've ever had while traveling?
16. What country or city do you recommend to everyone?
17. How do you handle homesickness when traveling?
18. What's the longest trip you've ever been on?
19. How does traveling affect your mental and physical health?
20. What are your essential travel items that you never leave without?
21. How do you choose your travel destinations?
22. What travel habit or ritual do you swear by?
23. What is the best travel advice you've ever received?
24. What do you always bring back from your travels?
25. How do you document and preserve your travel memories?
26. What lesser-known destination do you think more people should visit?
27. What's the most spontaneous trip you've ever taken?

28. How has your approach to travel changed over the years?

29. What travel-related goal are you most proud of achieving?

30. What has been your most meaningful interaction with a local while traveling?

31. How do you stay safe and secure when exploring a new place?

32. What do you think everyone should try at least once while traveling?

33. How do you make the most out of a short trip?

34. What's the biggest myth about traveling that you've found to be untrue?

35. How do you handle travel setbacks or plans that fall through?

36. What is the most interesting piece of history you've learned while traveling?

37. How do you approach eco-friendly travel?

38. What's the most unusual mode of transportation you've used on a trip?

39. How do you deal with jet lag and time changes?

40. What destination surprised you the most with its beauty?

41. What's the funniest or most embarrassing travel story you can share?

42. How has travel influenced your fashion or style?

43. What is your approach to budgeting for travel?

44. What historical landmark has made the biggest impression on you?

45. How do you make local friends or acquaintances while traveling?

46. What's the most useful thing you've learned from your travels?

47. How do you immerse yourself in the local culture of the places you visit?

48. What place have you visited that you would love to live in?

49. How has traveling alone differed from traveling with others?

50. What travel experience exceeded your expectations the most?

51. How do you deal with cultural shock?

52. What are the best and worst travel accommodations you've experienced?

53. What keepsake from your travels is most meaningful to you?

54. How do you discover hidden gems in a new city?

55. What's the most impactful book or film about travel that you've encountered?

56. How do you recharge after a long day of exploring?

57. What are your travel plans for the coming year?

58. How do you evaluate the success of a trip?

59. What's the most important lesson travel has taught you about yourself?

60. How do you share your travel experiences with others when you return home?

VOLUNTEERING AND CHARITY QUESTIONS

1. What was your first volunteering experience, and what did it teach you?

2. Why do you think volunteering is important?

3. What cause is closest to your heart, and why?

4. How do you choose which charities or organizations to support?

5. Describe a moment during volunteering that profoundly impacted you.

6. How has your view on charity and philanthropy evolved over time?

7. What skills have you gained from your volunteering experiences?

8. How do you balance your time between work, personal life, and volunteering?

9. Have you ever started a charitable initiative? Tell us about it.

10. What is the biggest challenge you've faced while volunteering?

11. How do you encourage others to get involved in volunteering?

12. What's the most creative fundraising idea you've taken part in or heard about?

13. How has volunteering influenced your career or professional life?

14. What misconceptions do people often have about volunteering?

15. How do you measure the impact of your volunteer work?

16. What are your criteria for choosing a charity to donate to?

17. How do you incorporate volunteer work into your family life?

18. What is the most urgent issue in your community that needs volunteers?

19. Have you ever been significantly changed by your volunteer work? How?

20. What advice would you give someone who wants to volunteer?

21. What are the benefits of volunteering that are rarely talked about?

22. How do you motivate yourself to volunteer regularly?

23. What role do you typically take on in volunteer projects?

24. Describe a volunteering experience abroad, if any. What did it involve?

25. What are your long-term goals regarding charity and volunteering?

26. How has volunteering helped you understand different cultures or communities?

27. What is the most significant donation you have ever made, and what prompted it?

28. How do you ensure the organizations you support are effective and transparent?

29. What type of volunteer work do you find most fulfilling?

30. How do you get your workplace involved in volunteering?

31. What local charity do you think deserves more recognition and support?

32. How has technology changed the way you engage with charity work?

33. What books or documentaries have influenced your views on charity and volunteering?

34. How do you handle feelings of burnout from volunteering?

35. What's a charity event you look forward to each year?

36. How do you spread awareness about the causes you care about?

37. What is a recent success story from your volunteering efforts?

38. How do you deal with the emotional impact of working in challenging volunteer roles?

39. What is the smallest act of kindness you believe has the biggest impact?

40. How has volunteering affected your personal relationships?

41. What skills or resources do you think are most needed in the volunteering sector?

42. Have you influenced someone to start volunteering? How?

43. What challenges do charities face that the public might not be aware of?

44. How do you react when you disagree with the policies of the organization you volunteer for?

45. What upcoming volunteer activities are you most excited about?

46. How do you involve your children or family in charity work?

47. What project or initiative have you volunteered for that is outside your comfort zone?

48. How do you celebrate the achievements and milestones of your volunteer team?

49. What has been your most humbling experience while volunteering?

50. How do you keep track of the various organizations and causes you support?

51. What has volunteering taught you about leadership?

52. How do you prioritize which events or causes to volunteer for when time is limited?

53. Describe a time when volunteering helped you make new friends or professional contacts.

54. What is the role of social media in your volunteering activities?

55. How do you follow up on the progress of the projects or people you've helped?

56. What's the biggest misconception you had about volunteering before you started?

57. How do you ensure that your contributions to charity are used as intended?

58. What is the most innovative volunteering or charity project you've seen or been a part of?

59. How has volunteering changed the way you see the world?

60. What legacy do you hope to leave through your charitable efforts?

LAW AND JUSTICE QUESTIONS

1. What does justice mean to you personally?

2. Have you ever had to seek legal advice? What was the situation?

3. What is one law you would change if you had the power, and why?

4. How do you define fairness in everyday situations?

5. Have you ever witnessed a situation where justice was not served? What impact did that have on you?

6. What are your thoughts on the death penalty?

7. How has the media shaped your understanding of law and justice?

8. What legal system from another country do you admire, and why?

9. Do you believe laws should evolve with society, or remain fixed once established?

10. What's the most significant court case you've ever followed? What drew you to it?

11. Has anyone wrongly accused you or someone close to you of something? How was the situation resolved?

12. How do you react when you see an injustice?

13. What role do you think ethics play in business?

14. How would you handle being on a jury for a serious crime?

15. What's your view on privacy laws and surveillance by the government?

16. How do you think your country's justice system could be improved?

17. Have you ever participated in a protest or movement seeking legal reform? What was the issue?

18. What's the most important legal protection that individuals should have?

19. How do you feel about the legalization of marijuana, either recreational or medicinal?

20. What are your thoughts on international law and organizations like the United Nations?

21. How does the justice system in your country handle issues of discrimination?

22. What experience have you had with law enforcement that shaped your view of the police?

23. How do you balance your personal feelings with legal obligations in difficult situations?

24. What's your stance on intellectual property rights?

25. Have you ever been involved in a legal contract negotiation? What did you learn?

26. What do you think about the bail system?

27. How important is the right to a fair trial to you?

28. Have you or someone you know ever been a victim of a crime? How was the aftermath handled?

29. What is your opinion on juvenile justice and the treatment of minors in the legal system?

30. How do you feel about the use of plea bargains in the judicial process?

31. What law or legal principle do you find most confusing, and why?

32. How do you feel about the concept of sovereign immunity?

33. What are your thoughts on the right to protest?

34. How do you feel about legal strategies that corporations use to minimize taxes?

35. What is your opinion on the role of international courts and tribunals?

36. How do you think history will judge current laws and legal practices?

37. Have you ever felt that you had to act as a mediator in a dispute? What was the outcome?

38. What are your thoughts on animal rights laws?

39. How do you feel about the legal implications of artificial intelligence and technology?

40. Do you think that environmental laws are sufficient in your country?

41. What is one historical legal figure you admire, and why?

42. How do you feel about the use of DNA evidence in solving crimes?

43. Have you ever had to testify in court? What was that experience like?

44. How do you feel about the patent system and its impact on innovation?

45. What are your thoughts on the legal system's handling of mental health issues?

46. How would you reform the prison system, if given the chance?

47. What legal fact or loophole surprised you when you learned about it?

48. How do you think your local community could improve its approach to law and order?

49. What do you believe is the biggest flaw in the criminal justice system today?

50. How has your personal background influenced your views on law and justice?

51. What are your thoughts on mandatory sentencing laws?

52. Have you ever used legal services for personal or business reasons? What was your experience?

53. How do you view the balance between freedom of speech and preventing hate speech?

54. What are your thoughts on the relationship between law enforcement and community engagement?

55. Have you ever been to a court hearing? What did you take away from the experience?

56. How do you think technology will change law enforcement in the future?

57. What legal advice would you give your younger self?

58. How do you view the ethics of legal practices in media and entertainment?

59. What impact do you think social movements have on changing laws?

60. How do you think laws regarding cyber security should evolve?

INTERNET AND SOCIAL MEDIA QUESTIONS

1. How has social media affected your relationships with friends and family?
2. What do you think are the biggest benefits of the internet?
3. Have you ever taken a break from social media? What prompted it and what did you learn?
4. How do you manage your privacy online?
5. What role does social media play in your daily routine?
6. How do you decide what to share and what to keep private on social media?
7. What's the most positive experience you've had online?
8. How has the internet changed the way you learn new things?
9. Do you think social media improves or worsens political discussions? Why?
10. What's your go-to app when you first wake up, and why?
11. Have you ever changed your opinion because of something you saw online? What was it about?
12. What internet resource is most valuable to you?
13. How do you feel about the amount of time you spend online daily?
14. Have you ever met someone in person who you first met online? Describe that experience.
15. What's the most surprising thing you've learned from online videos or tutorials?
16. How do you feel about the future of digital communication?
17. What measures do you take to secure your data and personal information online?
18. How do you think the internet will evolve in the next ten years?
19. What's the worst piece of advice you've seen shared widely on social media?
20. How has social media influenced your shopping habits?
21. What is your perspective on internet celebrities and influencers?
22. How do you differentiate between credible and questionable sources online?
23. How has social media affected your self-esteem or body image?
24. What's the most controversial topic you've discussed online?
25. How do you handle online disagreements?
26. What is one thing you wish everyone knew about social media?
27. How has the internet helped you connect with like-minded individuals?
28. What do you think about the spread of misinformation on the internet?
29. How has the internet impacted your career or professional life?
30. What's the funniest or most entertaining content you regularly follow online?
31. Do you take part in any online communities or forums? What draws you to them?
32. What was the last thing you Googled, and why?
33. How do you balance online interactions with face-to-face relationships?
34. What's the most memorable online event you participated in?
35. How do you use the internet to relax or de-stress?
36. Have you ever contributed to an online charity or crowdfunding campaign? What motivated you?
37. What's one online trend that you don't understand or appreciate?
38. How do you think virtual and augmented reality will change social media?

39. What are the ethical considerations of posting about others, including children, on social media?

40. How do you feel about the permanence of the digital content you create?

41. Have you ever regretted something you've posted online? What was it?

42. What's the most useful online tool or service you've discovered?

43. How do you decide who to follow or unfollow on social media?

44. How do you feel about the role of algorithms in shaping your online experience?

45. What's your favorite way to consume news: online, print, TV, or radio?

46. How has the internet influenced your understanding of different cultures?

47. What online habit would you like to change or improve?

48. What's the biggest lesson you've learned about human nature from online interactions?

49. How do you see artificial intelligence impacting your internet use in the future?

50. What's the most significant way the internet has affected your hobbies or personal interests?

51. How do you maintain focus and productivity with the distractions of the internet?

52. What do you think about the accessibility of the internet across the globe?

53. How has the internet influenced your health, either positively or negatively?

54. What's the most compelling story you've followed through online news?

55. What concerns you most about your children's or future generations' internet use?

56. How do you use the internet to make your everyday life easier or more efficient?

57. What online resource do you think is underutilized?

58. How has the anonymity of the internet affected your behavior or others'?

59. What steps do you take to disconnect and unplug from digital media?

60. How do you think the balance between online and offline life will change in the future?

RETIREMENT AND AGING QUESTIONS

1. What does aging gracefully mean to you?

2. How do you plan to stay physically and mentally active in retirement?

3. What are your biggest concerns about retirement?

4. How has your perspective on aging changed as you've gotten older?

5. What are the most important lessons you've learned from older generations?

6. How do you feel about the financial aspects of your retirement planning?

7. What hobbies or activities do you look forward to pursuing in retirement?

8. What steps are you taking to ensure a healthy lifestyle as you age?

9. How do you plan to maintain social connections in retirement?

10. What legacy do you hope to leave behind for your family or community?

11. How do you deal with the physical changes that come with aging?

12. What are your thoughts on senior living options like retirement communities or assisted living?

13. How important is it to you to be financially independent in your older years?

14. What role do you see yourself playing in your family as you get older?

15. What are your plans for your living situation in retirement?

16. How do you prepare for potential health issues associated with aging?

17. What measures are you taking to protect your assets and estate as you age?

18. How do you feel about the possibility of needing long-term care?

19. What traditions or values do you want to pass on to future generations?

20. How do you cope with the loss of friends and loved ones as you age?

21. What has been your biggest surprise about getting older?

22. How do you keep your mind sharp and engaged?

23. What are your thoughts on volunteering or working part-time in retirement?

24. How do you approach discussions about end-of-life care and preferences?

25. What do you find most rewarding about growing older?

26. What advice would you give to someone younger about preparing for old age?

27. How do you manage stress and anxiety about the future?

28. What are your goals for personal development in later life?

29. How has your relationship with technology adapted as you've aged?

30. What are your strategies for maintaining your independence as long as possible?

31. How do you celebrate significant age milestones?

32. What is your favorite memory related to an older family member or friend?

33. How do you feel about the aging process being portrayed in media and culture?

34. What changes have you made to your home to accommodate aging?

35. How do you stay informed about health advancements and age-related research?

36. What are the benefits of your current age?

37. How do you handle the generational gap with younger family members?

38. What do you enjoy most about your current stage of life?

39. How has your diet and nutrition changed as you've gotten older?

40. What do you miss most about your youth?

41. How do you handle the emotional aspects of retirement (e.g., loss of professional identity)?

42. What kind of travel do you hope to do during retirement?

43. What have you learned about friendship in your later years?

44. How do you feel about the representation of elderly people in politics and leadership?

45. What has been the impact of retirement on your marriage or significant relationships?

46. How do you manage the balance between independence and accepting help as you age?

47. What are your favorite ways to pass on knowledge and experience to younger generations?

48. How do you approach the use of medications and interventions in aging?

49. What role does spirituality or religion play in your thoughts on aging?

50. How have your priorities shifted as you've aged?

51. What activities or routines have you found essential for your well-being in older age?

52. How do you deal with changes in mobility or physical capabilities?

53. What are your thoughts on life after retirement?

54. How do you celebrate your achievements and life milestones now?

55. How do you approach aging with humor and positivity?

56. What misconceptions about aging do you frequently encounter?

57. How has your sense of style or personal expression evolved as you've aged?

58. What are the biggest challenges you face with technology as you grow older?

59. What gives you joy and fulfillment in your later years?

60. How do you see your role within your community as you age?

BUSINESS AND ENTREPRENEURSHIP QUESTIONS

1. What inspired you to enter the field of business or entrepreneurship?

2. Describe the first business idea you ever had, whether or not you pursued it.

3. What has been your biggest challenge as an entrepreneur or business professional?

4. How do you handle risk and uncertainty in business decisions?

5. What is the most valuable lesson you've learned from a business failure?

6. How do you define success in business?

7. What personal qualities do you think are most important for entrepreneurial success?

8. How has your approach to business changed over time?

9. What business leader do you most admire, and why?

10. How do you foster innovation within your business or team?

11. What's the best piece of business advice you've ever received?

12. Describe a time when you had to make a tough business decision.

13. How do you balance ethical considerations with profitability?

14. What strategies have you found most effective for promoting your business?

15. How do you handle competition in your industry?

16. What was a pivotal moment of growth for your business, and how did it come about?

17. How do you manage stress and maintain a work-life balance?

18. What role does customer feedback play in your business model?

19. How do you cultivate a positive company culture?

20. What new skills have you had to learn to enhance your business acumen?

21. Describe a significant setback you've experienced in business and how you overcame it.

22. How do you stay motivated during tough times in your business?

23. What emerging trends in your industry excite you the most?

24. What does a typical day look like for you as an entrepreneur or business leader?

25. How do you prepare for a big presentation or business meeting?

26. What book on business or leadership has profoundly affected you?

27. How do you measure the impact of your business on your community or industry?

28. What was the most rewarding moment in your business career?

29. How do you approach networking and building professional relationships?

30. What's the biggest risk you've taken in your career?

31. How has technology changed the way you do business?

32. What is one business you would love to start if resources were no object?

33. How do you stay updated with industry news and advancements?

34. What are the core values that drive your business decisions?

35. How do you handle feedback and criticism?

36. What is the most challenging aspect of managing employees?

37. How do you ensure your business adapts to changing market conditions?

38. What strategies do you use to keep your team motivated and productive?

39. What do you find most fulfilling about running a business?

40. How do you prioritize tasks and manage your time effectively?

41. Describe a time when you had to innovate to solve a problem.

42. How do you incorporate social responsibility into your business practices?

43. What advice would you give to a new entrepreneur?

44. What financial management strategies have been crucial for your business?

45. How do you approach scaling your business?

46. What impact has mentoring had on your professional journey?

47. How do you handle disagreements or conflicts within your team?

48. What industry-specific conferences or seminars have you found most beneficial?

49. How do you maintain energy and passion for your work?

50. What legal or regulatory challenges have you faced in your business?

51. How do you manage the emotional highs and lows of entrepreneurship?

52. What personal sacrifices have you made to ensure your business's success?

53. How do you determine the viability of a new business idea?

54. What role does intuition play in your business decisions?

55. How do you approach outsourcing or delegating tasks?

56. What strategies have you implemented to improve customer loyalty?

57. How do you ensure transparency in your business operations?

58. What's the most unexpected challenge you've faced in business?

59. How do you plan for retirement as an entrepreneur?

60. What legacy do you hope to leave through your business endeavors?

HOLIDAYS AND FESTIVITIES QUESTIONS

1. What is your favorite holiday and why?

2. Describe a family tradition that you cherish during the holidays.

3. How has your way of celebrating major holidays changed over the years?

4. Which holiday do you think is overrated, and why?

5. What's the best holiday gift you've ever received?

6. Have you ever traveled during the holidays? Where did you go and what did you experience?

7. What's your favorite holiday movie or song, and what memories are associated with it?

8. How do you usually decorate for the festive season?

9. What holiday from another culture do you find fascinating, and why?

10. How do you handle holiday stress?

11. What's the most memorable New Year's Eve you've ever had?

12. Have you ever volunteered during the holidays? What was that experience like?

13. What does the spirit of giving mean to you during the holidays?

14. Describe a holiday you dislike and why.
15. What festive food or drink do you look forward to all year?
16. Have you ever hosted a holiday party? Share how it went.
17. What's a holiday that you think deserves more recognition?
18. How do you save or budget for holiday spending?
19. What holiday traditions have you started yourself?
20. How do holidays affect your feelings about family and togetherness?
21. Have you ever had a holiday mishap? What happened?
22. What's your favorite part of the holiday season?
23. How do you feel about the commercialization of certain holidays?
24. Do you make New Year's resolutions? How successful are you in keeping them?
25. What's the best holiday-themed event you've ever attended?
26. Describe a holiday you celebrated differently because of circumstances like travel or living abroad.
27. How do holidays impact your religious or spiritual beliefs?
28. What's the weirdest holiday tradition you've ever heard of or experienced?
29. How do you reconnect with friends and family during the holidays?
30. What's your approach to gift-giving?
31. Do you have a favorite holiday decoration, and what is its story?
32. How do major holidays impact your mental health?
33. What's the most thoughtful gift you've ever given?
34. Describe your ideal way to spend a holiday.
35. Have you ever experienced a holiday in a completely different climate (e.g., Christmas on the beach)?
36. How do you handle differences in holiday traditions when celebrating with others?
37. What holiday do you find the most challenging, and why?
38. Have you ever forgotten an important holiday? What was the outcome?
39. What's your favorite holiday memory from childhood?
40. How do you incorporate charity or giving back into your holiday traditions?
41. What holiday rituals are important in your workplace or community?
42. How do you deal with loneliness during the holidays?
43. What's the most unusual holiday gift you've ever received?
44. How does the change in seasons affect your holiday celebrations?
45. Do you prefer a quiet holiday or a festive, busy one?
46. How do you recover from the hustle and bustle of the holiday season?
47. What lessons have you learned about yourself during holiday gatherings?
48. Do you prefer traditional holiday meals or like to experiment with new recipes?
49. What's your strategy for dealing with unwanted holiday invitations?
50. How do you manage expectations during the holidays?
51. What aspects of the holidays do you find magical or inspirational?
52. Have you ever had a holiday romance? Describe that experience.
53. How do you keep alive the memory of loved ones during the holidays?

54. What are your thoughts on gift cards as holiday presents?

55. How do you manage holiday traditions from different sides of your family?

56. What holiday has the most personal meaning to you, and why?

57. How do you ensure that you keep true to the meaning of the holiday season?

58. Describe a holiday craft or project you particularly enjoyed.

59. What have been your most significant realizations during festive reflections?

60. How do you want to improve or change your holiday celebrations in the future?

MORAL AND ETHICAL DILEMMAS QUESTIONS

1. Describe a time when you faced a moral dilemma at work. What did you decide?

2. How do you determine what is right and wrong in a complex situation?

3. Have you ever had to compromise your ethics for professional advancement? How did it make you feel?

4. What do you believe is more important: loyalty to friends or loyalty to principles?

5. How do you handle situations where your ethical beliefs conflict with someone else's?

6. What ethical issue in today's society concerns you the most?

7. If you found a wallet full of cash, what would you do and why?

8. How do you decide when to break a rule or law?

9. What's an example of a justified lie in your opinion?

10. How do you deal with people whose ethical views radically differ from yours?

11. Is it ever okay to sacrifice one life to save others? Under what circumstances?

12. How do you prioritize competing ethical principles when making decisions?

13. What are your thoughts on the death penalty?

14. How would you handle a situation where following orders conflicts with your moral beliefs?

15. How do you incorporate ethical considerations into your daily life?

16. What role does forgiveness play in your moral and ethical worldview?

17. What's your stance on using animals in scientific research?

18. How do you reconcile personal benefit with potential harm to others?

19. What would you do if you discovered a friend doing something unethical?

20. How do you balance personal privacy with the need for security or surveillance?

21. Would you report unethical behavior if it could harm your career?

22. What do you consider unforgivable?

23. How does your cultural background influence your moral decisions?

24. What would you do if someone asked you to keep a secret that you believed should be revealed for someone's safety?

25. How do you approach ethical consumption in your lifestyle choices?

26. How does empathy influence your ethical decisions?

27. Is it ever ethical to prioritize the needs of the many over the needs of the few?

28. What do you believe is the root cause of most ethical dilemmas in modern society?

29. How would you advise someone facing an ethical dilemma?

30. How has your approach to ethical dilemmas changed as you've aged?
31. What historical figure do you believe exemplified moral integrity?
32. How do you think technology affects our understanding of ethics?
33. What ethical challenges do you foresee arising from future technological advancements?
34. How do you manage the tension between ethical ideals and practical realities?
35. Do you think individuals learn ethical behavior or are born with it?
36. What ethical issue do you think lacks sufficient attention?
37. How do you navigate ethical issues in social media and online interactions?
38. What role should ethics play in business and government?
39. Have you ever taken a stand that was unpopular but you felt was right?
40. How do ethical considerations affect your financial decisions?
41. What's the most significant ethical lesson you've learned from your parents?
42. How do you respond when personal and professional ethics collide?
43. What's an example of a modern ethical issue you find particularly challenging?
44. How do you evaluate the ethics of a company or organization before supporting them?
45. What is your perspective on whistleblowing?
46. How do you think society can improve its collective ethical standards?
47. What's a personal rule you never break?
48. How do you feel about the ethical implications of cloning and genetic editing?
49. What measures do you take to ensure you act ethically in tough situations?
50. How do you teach ethical principles to younger generations?
51. What ethical dilemma from a book or film deeply affected you, and why?
52. How do you think differing ethical standards should be reconciled in a globalized world?
53. What do you believe is the biggest ethical challenge facing the youth today?
54. How do you ensure fairness in your interactions with others?
55. What steps do you take when you realize you've made an unethical decision?
56. How do you deal with situations where there's no clear ethical choice?
57. What questions do you ask yourself when faced with a difficult ethical decision?
58. How do you hold yourself accountable for your ethical decisions?
59. In what ways do you lead by example in terms of ethics?
60. How do you cope with the aftermath of ethical dilemmas?

GLOBAL ISSUES AND AWARENESS QUESTIONS

1. What global issue do you feel most passionate about?
2. How do you stay informed about international news?
3. What role do you believe you play in solving global problems?
4. How can individuals contribute to global economic development?
5. What's your stance on climate change and personal responsibility?
6. How can we balance economic growth with environmental sustainability?
7. In what ways can education combat global inequality?

8. What do you think is the most pressing health crisis the world faces today?

9. How can the average person support peace in conflict-ridden areas?

10. What are the ethical implications of international trade policies?

11. How do you think travel influences global awareness?

12. What's the impact of digital connectivity on global relations?

13. How can we address the global digital divide?

14. What are the consequences of ignoring international humanitarian crises?

15. How can art and culture bridge global divides?

16. What is the role of social media in shaping global opinions?

17. How should the international community handle refugees?

18. What's your take on the importance of preserving world heritage sites?

19. How do global pandemics change your perspective on health and wellness?

20. What do you think about the role of international organizations like the UN?

21. Can one person make a difference in global issues?

22. What's your understanding of fair trade and its impact?

23. How can technology be used to solve global problems?

24. What global issue do you think is underreported?

25. How do you see the future of global food security?

26. What changes can you make in your daily life to support sustainability?

27. How do you think cultural differences affect global communication?

28. What steps can governments take to improve global literacy?

29. How can we ensure water access and cleanliness for all?

30. What are your thoughts on the intersection of politics and global health?

31. How can we as individuals support ethical consumption?

32. What does it mean to be a global citizen?

33. How does tourism impact global economies and environments?

34. What can be done to protect endangered species on a global scale?

35. What are your views on global gun control laws?

36. How can we address the global challenges of aging populations?

37. In what ways can we foster global cultural exchanges?

38. How can individuals support disaster relief efforts abroad?

39. What are the moral implications of international adoption?

40. How do advances in global communication shape our world?

41. What's the most effective way to engage in global volunteerism?

42. How do trade tariffs affect you or your country?

43. What is the impact of global warming on small communities?

44. How can countries work together to combat cyber threats?

45. What personal changes are you willing to make to combat climate change?

46. How does language shape our understanding of global issues?

47. What can the younger generation do to influence global policy?

48. How do international sports events promote unity?

49. What role should multinational corporations play in social responsibility?

50. How does your country's foreign policy affect its citizens?

51. What are the global implications of space exploration?

52. How can we globally reduce our reliance on non-renewable energy sources?

53. What are the benefits and risks of global economic interdependence?

54. How can we better support countries facing famine and drought?

55. What do you believe is the key to achieving world peace?

56. How does globalization affect your local job market?

57. What are the ethical considerations of medical research in developing countries?

58. How can you be more environmentally friendly in your community?

59. What are the pros and cons of global standardization?

60. How can you practice cultural sensitivity in a globalized world?

INNOVATION AND FUTURE TRENDS QUESTIONS

1. What emerging technology do you think will most impact the future?

2. How do you stay up-to-date with the latest innovations?

3. Which future trend excites you the most?

4. What are the ethical implications of artificial intelligence?

5. How could virtual reality change our daily lives?

6. What potential do you see in renewable energy technologies?

7. How do you envision the future of transportation?

8. What role do you think robots should have in society?

9. How can we prepare for the jobs of the future?

10. What's your biggest concern about the impact of new technology on privacy?

11. How do you think the education system should adapt to future trends?

12. What's your vision for the future of healthcare?

13. In what ways can technology enhance our personal lives?

14. How do you see the evolution of human communication with tech advancements?

15. What safeguards should be in place for genetic editing technologies?

16. Can technology solve the issues of food scarcity and distribution?

17. What innovations do you think could revolutionize the workplace?

18. How can society address the digital divide as we move towards the future?

19. What are your thoughts on the sustainability of cryptocurrency?

20. How do you feel about the ethical use of drones in civilian life?

21. How should humanity approach the possibility of colonizing other planets?

22. In what ways do you think artificial intelligence could shape creativity?

23. What do you think will be the next big breakthrough in science?

24. How will advancements in technology impact human relationships?

25. What role will technology play in the future of education?

26. How might technology impact the way we govern in the future?

27. What do you think will be the biggest change in how we consume media?

28. How can we ensure that technology will be used ethically in the future?

29. What do you hope technology will never change about humanity?

30. How will the advancement of technology affect our concept of work-life balance?

31. What skills do you think will be most valuable in a technologically advanced future?

32. What innovation do you think will significantly extend human lifespan?

33. How do you feel about the integration of technology into the human body?

34. What are the risks and benefits of creating more smart cities?

35. How might technology reshape our approach to global crises?

36. What do you think will be the role of human intuition in a data-driven future?

37. How should we prepare for the impact of automation on employment?

38. What changes do you anticipate in the structure of the family due to technology?

39. What's your opinion on the potential for technology to bridge cultural gaps?

40. How will e-commerce and delivery technology evolve in the coming years?

41. What are the implications of biotechnology in food production?

42. How do you perceive the future of social media and its influence on society?

43. What role will machine learning play in personalizing education?

44. How can we maintain a sense of community in an increasingly virtual world?

45. What's your stance on the use of technology in maintaining public safety and security?

46. What do you think will be the most surprising technological change in the next decade?

47. How can technology help in the preservation of the environment?

48. What ethical guidelines should be in place for experimenting with brain-computer interfaces?

49. How might augmented reality change professional training and development?

50. What do you think is the future of entertainment with emerging technologies?

51. How can technology be leveraged to create a more equitable society?

52. What are your thoughts on the personalization of healthcare through technology?

53. How should the legal system evolve to address cyber-law in the future?

54. What are the potential consequences of a globally connected Internet of Things?

55. How do you see technology shaping the future of art and expression?

56. How can technology enhance the democratic process?

57. What innovations do you predict will revolutionize travel and exploration?

58. What are the social implications of increasingly sophisticated simulation technologies?

59. How will advancements in technology change human physical abilities?

60. What will be the most critical ethical considerations in a technologically advanced society?

DEATH AND AFTERLIFE QUESTIONS

1. What are your beliefs about what happens after death?

2. How do you cope with the fear of death, if you experience it?

3. Have you ever had a near-death experience? What was it like?

4. What do you think are the most comforting words to say to someone who is grieving?

5. How do you want to be remembered after you pass away?

6. What song would you choose to be played at your funeral and why?

7. Have you ever attended a funeral that particularly moved you? What made it memorable?

8. How do you honor the memory of someone who has died?

9. Do you believe in signs or messages from the afterlife? Have you ever received one?

10. How has your view of death changed as you've gotten older?

11. What do you think is important to achieve or experience before you die?

12. Have you ever written a will? What prompted you to do so?

13. Do you prefer burial, cremation, or another method after death?

14. What is your most cherished memory of someone who has passed away?

15. How do you deal with the anniversaries of loved ones' deaths?

16. What book, movie, or artwork about death has significantly affected you?

17. Do you talk openly about death with your family or friends? Why or why not?

18. What traditions or customs from your culture around death do you find most meaningful?

19. How would you want to spend your last day if you knew when it was coming?

20. What do you think makes a good life, considering our mortality?

21. How do you approach the concept of legacy and leaving something behind?

22. What fears do you have regarding the process of dying?

23. How does your spirituality or religion influence your views on the afterlife?

24. Have you ever planned your funeral? What details did you decide on?

25. What lessons have you learned from the deaths of others?

26. How do you want people to celebrate your life after you're gone?

27. What practical preparations have you made for your death (e.g., life insurance, funeral plans)?

28. How do you perceive the relationship between life and death?

29. What ethical considerations around death (e.g., euthanasia) do you feel strongly about?

30. Have you ever experienced a profound sense of peace when thinking about death?

31. What do you think about the idea of an afterlife or reincarnation?

32. How do you make sense of the death of young or innocent people?

33. What impact has the death of public figures or celebrities had on you?

34. Have you ever helped someone through their grieving process? What did you learn?

35. What questions do you hope to have answered about life after you die?

36. How has the loss of a pet affected your views on death and mourning?

37. What are your thoughts on the rituals that follow death in different cultures?

38. How does nature's life cycle influence your thoughts on human death?

39. Have you ever took part in a death cafe or discussion group about mortality?

40. What personal growth have you experienced because of contemplating death?

41. How do you find comfort when thinking about death?

42. What are your thoughts on preserving memories for future generations?

43. How do you reconcile the death of someone who did not share your beliefs about the afterlife?

44. What are the most challenging aspects of discussing death with children?

45. How do you manage your digital legacy?

46. What role do you think grief plays in understanding death?

47. How do you view the medical profession's role in the process of dying?

48. What do you find most challenging about the concept of eternity?

49. How do you think society's view of death and dying has changed over time?

50. What innovations around death and dying have you heard about that interest you (e.g., green burials)?

51. How do you deal with existential dread related to death?

52. What are your thoughts on the death penalty?

53. How do you support friends or family members who have a terminal illness?

54. What are your hopes for your final years of life?

55. How does art help you process your feelings about death?

56. What are your thoughts on mourning practices and periods?

57. How do you practice mindfulness in the face of mortality?

58. What do you think is the societal impact of avoiding discussions about death?

59. How do you maintain hope and positivity in life with the inevitability of death?

60. What experiences have you had that reaffirmed your beliefs about what happens after death?

Final Words

As you turn to the final pages of "3000 Powerful Questions About Myself" it's important to pause and reflect on the journey you've undertaken. This book was produced not just to ask questions but to provoke thought, inspire introspection, and challenge your perceptions about who you are and what shapes your life.

Reflections on the Journey:

Through this series of questions, you've explored various facets of your identity, delved into your deepest fears, celebrated your triumphs, and perhaps unearthed desires you hadn't acknowledged before. Each question was a step deeper into your own psyche, a probe into the complex structure of your thoughts and feelings.

The Power of Questions:

What makes a question powerful is not just what it asks, but what it unveils. Questions are the keys that unlock doors within us, doors to rooms we may not have realized existed. This exploration is not about finding the right answers but about discovering truths—your truths. And in your responses, you've likely found more than just facts; you've uncovered emotions, memories, and perhaps even new dreams.

Continued Exploration:

The end of this book does not signify the end of your journey. Consider how you might keep the spirit of inquiry alive:

- **Revisit your answers:** Over time, your responses may evolve as you do. Revisiting your answers can provide insight into how you've changed and what remains a constant in your life.
- **Pose new questions:** As your life unfolds, new questions will naturally arise. Continue to ask, explore, and reflect. Use the skills you've honed here to engage with these new inquiries.
- **Share the journey:** Consider sharing this book with friends, family, or even colleagues. Discussing your answers can deepen your relationships and offer new perspectives on shared experiences.

The Impact of Reflection:

Reflection is a powerful tool for growth. By questioning our lives, we can live more intentionally and with greater awareness. The insights you've gained here can inform your decisions, enrich your relationships, and enhance your understanding of your own life narrative.

Final Thoughts:

"3000 Powerful Questions About Myself" is more than a book—it's a companion on a voyage to the heart of who you are. Thank you for embracing this journey with openness and courage. May the questions you've answered inspire you to continue asking, exploring, and growing. And remember, every question you've explored is a part of the larger conversation with yourself, one that continues as long as you keep asking.

Keep questioning, keep discovering, and above all, keep celebrating the unique story that is your life.

A Quick Favor to Ask

I'd like to please kindly ask you to leave me a review. Please leave me a review as I don't have the same budget as big publishing companies and your input would be highly appreciated.

To leave your review of this book, please scan this QR code:

Your support will mean a lot to me, and I thank you in advance for your help!

Mauricio

Made in the USA
Monee, IL
22 November 2024

70932329R00052